Dec. 31st. 1949.

THE DELPHINIUM

In the Same Series
THE DIANTHUS by Will Ingwersen

In Preparation
THE PRIMULA by Walter E. Th. Ingwersen
THE LUPIN by Tom Reeves
ANNUALS by A. P. Boissier

*

General Editor
A. P. BOISSIER

THE DELPHINIUM

A FLOWER MONOGRAPH

By

FRANK BISHOP

COLLINS

ST JAMES'S PLACE LONDON

1949

To
My Dear Wife

CONTENTS

*

CONTENTS

COLOUR PLATES

MONOCHROME ILLUSTRATIONS

ACKNOWLEDGMENTS FOR
ILLUSTRATIONS

*

Mr. Michael Haworth-Booth : I-III, V-IX, 9, 15

Reginald A. Malby & Co. : 2, 3, 4, 5, 8

The Engraving Co. Ltd.,
Wolverhampton : IV, 6, 7, 10, 12, 13, 14

Amateur Gardening : 11

FOREWORD

★

FOR some time past we have felt that there was a need in garden literature for a series of monographs each of which dealt with a particular genus of plants, and which were written by authors who had made a careful and practical study of their subject. Experience has taught us that nowadays the gardening public wish to know more and more about the flowers they grow, their origin, their variety, their likes and dislikes. In order to meet this need this present series is being undertaken, and it is believed that it will be welcomed by all to whom gardening is a joy, as well as by those to whom it is a business.

Mr. Bishop has been an enthusiastic gardener for many years. Sweet Peas first attracted his attention and, after reading R. C. Punnett's book on " Mendelism," he became bitten with the idea of raising his own seedlings. This he did, and bred several of outstanding merit. Unfortunately, the first World War put an end to this activity, and on his return he found that all his seedlings had disappeared.

However, it is a very ill wind that does not bring some good in its train. Shortly after his demobilisation he became enamoured of the Delphinium, and, starting with a few named varieties, he was soon showing his blooms at the British Delphinium Society's shows, and with them he won many cups and prizes.

It was inevitable that once he had become a successful exhibitor, the desire to breed new varieties should follow. Each year he studied the exhibits displayed, and rapidly came to the conclusion that the pure blue varieties were not only few in number, but were also neither comparable in size nor habit with the mauves and other shades. The idea of producing a good blue strain appealed strongly to him, so, setting to work, he has after some sixteen years of cross-fertilization and selection produced a strain of pure blue delphiniums which are equal to the best varieties in other colours. During that time he has received from the Royal Horticultural Society over thirty Awards of Merit for outstanding forms.

He therefore brings to this book a knowledge gained not only through his unbounded enthusiasm, but also from the experience he has gathered through the practical work he has done.

A. P. BOISSIER
General Editor

CHAPTER I

HISTORY

*

FEW people can resist the appeal of the modern delphinium with its spires of blue that rival even the gentians in their brilliance of colour, but how many pause to consider where it originated and who set in motion the fusion of the species that has culminated in these masterpieces of the breeder's art. These modern monarchs are the result of the hybridization of numerous species that are found all over the world, but it is not known who was responsible for the pioneer work. Nor is anything very definite known about the species that were used for hybridizing, although we are fairly certain that one of the forerunners was a blue species from the Swiss Alps, *D. elatum* (from *elatus*, meaning tall), which grows up to a height of 6 ft. Present day delphiniums resemble *D. elatum* in habit, build and foliage and for these reasons are known as " elatum " type delphiniums. *D. cheilanthum*, a dark blue Siberian species with a yellow eye, is also believed to have been used. Probably we have to thank, or rather curse, this species for the mildew that attacks so many of our present day varieties. We conjecture that other species employed were *D. brunonianum* from the Himalayas, purple violet in colour and hooded in form, and *D. formosum* from Armenia. Doubtless there have been many others which would account for the diversity of form and colour in the present day hybrids, but we know nothing for certain.

Delphiniums received their name from the ancient Greeks who, by some stretch of the imagination, saw a resemblance in the delphinium bud to a dolphin. In England in Tudor times species and annual delphiniums were popular. They were alluded to as Larkspurs, because the nectary, that part of the flower that secrets the nectar, was thought to resemble the spur of a lark's claw. It was about three hundred years ago that the *elatum* type came into general cultivation. In 1640 John Parkinson, apothecary to Charles I, had a famous garden in London, and writing about the delphiniums then in cultivation mentioned *D. elatius flore plena*. Referring to their name he writes, " We call them in English, Larkes heeles, Larkes spurres, Larkes toes or clawes."

Although these hybrid delphiniums had been in cultivation since the seventeenth century no very great advance was made until about the middle of the nineteenth century when Mr. James Kelway, the founder of the famous Langport nurseries in Somerset, concentrated his efforts on improving the race. He procured the best available varieties, including many from France, and set to work to cross-fertilize them. Thousands of seedlings were grown, and careful selection soon resulted in varieties superior to any then in commerce. Many were exhibited and received Awards of Merit from the Royal Horticultural Society. In all, over 100 delphiniums raised by Kelways have been honoured by these Awards.

But great as was the progress accomplished by Kelway during the latter half of the nineteenth century, far greater strides were to be made in the years that followed. In 1904 Messrs. Blackmore and Langdon of Bath acquired the best varieties of Kelway, Lemoine and other raisers and began to breed a strain of delphiniums that was destined to make the firm world famous. In a few years a stream of varieties, superior in length and build of spike, size and form of floret, and finer in every respect than any seen before, began to flow from their nursery. Each succeeding year new colours and improvements on older varieties were introduced. To appreciate the amazing progress that was made

1. A modern White
   Delphinium

2. Showing how to stake and tie. (D. Tessa)

it is only necessary to compare the superb varieties of the present time with those in general cultivation prior to the first world war.

It is beyond doubt that the credit for raising the delphinium to its present state of perfection is mainly due to the systematic breeding carried out by Blackmore and Langdon following the pioneer work of Kelway. Nevertheless, other breeders, both amateur and professional, have played their parts in the development.

To cause a sensation with flowers at a Royal Horticultural Society show is no mean achievement, but that is what happened at a meeting on June 21st, 1921, when Mr. Watkin Samuel, of Wrexham, exhibited the first of his Wrexham delphiniums. Such huge spikes had never before been seen. The outstanding features of the Wrexham strain are the long pyramidal spikes tapering from a very broad base. Usually the stems are thick, and the rather widely spaced florets are carried on long pedicels. For the most part, the colours are mauves and purples with blue back sepals, but in recent years Mr. Samuel has produced some fine self-blue varieties. The fame of this strain, called by some " Hollyhock " delphiniums because of a supposed resemblance to that flower, quickly spread all over the world. American specialists imported large quantities of seed which they sold at high prices. The named varieties were mainly distributed in this country by three Midland specialist firms, Bakers of Codsall (of Russell Lupin fame), Bees of Chester, and Hewitts of Stratford on Avon, whose proprietor, Mr. George Phillips, is the author of the well-known book *Delphiniums*, published in 1933.

My own efforts at breeding delphiniums began in 1932, but limited space restricted the number of seedlings I was able to grow, and it was not until 1935, when I acquired a piece of ground from my next door neighbour, that I settled down in real earnest to carrying out my ambition. In the early days named varieties of other raisers were used in my crosses, but nothing outstanding resulted from the first few years work. I aimed at a high standard, and every seedling that fell short of that standard was ruthlessly destroyed. By 1936 I had accumulated a few good seedlings with distinctive features which I used for cross-fertilizing. By this time I had made up my mind to concentrate principally on developing blue varieties. With this object in view I carefully selected the parents for my crosses. One parent was usually pure blue, the other predominantly blue but with outstanding features in other directions. Apart from the colour, I selected those that excelled in size and build of spike, and size and form of floret, for by so doing I hoped eventually I should be able to blend the two types, but progress was slow. The pure blues that did come were no better than those I had used for parents, and the best of my seedlings were not blue. However, in 1938 a good blue seedling turned up. Although not the ideal blue I was seeking, it had many good points and was destined to be a parent of several good things to come. From that time steady progress has been made and now the pure blue strain I dreamed of is an accomplished fact.

In 1942 I met Mr. James Baker and discussed with him the question of his firm putting Bishop delphiniums on the market. We arrived at a satisfactory agreement, with the result that all the Bishop delphiniums are to be distributed by Messrs. Bakers of Codsall. Later, Mr. Baker suggested that much greater progress could be made if I would devote my whole time to delphinium development, so in February, 1946, I retired from business and joined Messrs. Bakers' staff at their Boningale nursery, where I now am wholly employed in growing and breeding delphiniums.

Although English breeders have been largely responsible for the great work that has been accomplished in raising the delphinium to the high position it now occupies in the horticultural world, much credit is also due to specialists in America and on the Continent. In America delphiniums are very popular, but methods differing from our own are employed in their culture. Whereas in England we generally grow named varieties, in America named varieties are practically non-existent. The extremes of heat and cold of the American climate tend to shorten the life of these plants. In some parts of the country they are perennial, while in others the climate is so unfavourable that they have to be treated as annuals or biennials. Consequently, as an alternative to distributing expensive named varieties which might die after once flowering, American breeders have concentrated on raising special strains of seed, such as Dr. Leon Leonian's Lyondel strain and Vetterly & Reinelt's Pacific strain, to mention only two of many.

White delphiniums have never been popular in England, but in America they are in great favour. The late Mr. Charles Barber, of Troutdale, Oregon, was the originator of the strain which became famous as the Hoodacre Whites. These have been further developed by Mr. Frank Reinelt, and distributed as the Galahad series. In habit the American whites are vigorous, growing from 5 to 8 ft. in height, with spikes and florets equal in size and form to the coloured varieties, but those who have given them a trial in England find that generally they are not as perennial as our own coloured varieties.

It is a matter for surprise that breeders in this country have done little or nothing about hybridizing the species, and, with the exception of Mr. Horace Knowles, of Great Barr, Birmingham, who has an extensive collection, very few gardeners cultivate them to any extent. Like the olden time seeker after the philosopher's stone, hybridizers have visions that have little chance of being realized. Among the elusive and possibly unattainable developments that figure in their dreams are Blue Roses, Yellow Sweet Peas, Blue Dahlias, Black Tulips and Blue Chrysanthemums. In the delphinium breeder's dream-garden of the future are majestic spikes of scarlet, orange, pink and yellow spikes comparable with the present day mauve and blue varieties.

To many such an alluring prospect may seem as impossible of attainment as are blue roses. Nevertheless, the dream is not as wild as it may appear, since all these colours exist in the species ; moreover small advances have already been made towards breeding them into new types, which may eventually result in the dream being realized.

Foremost in the work of developing this new colour range into delphiniums are breeders in America who have better facilities than we have in this country, since America is the native habitat of numerous species, including the scarlet *D. cardinale*, from which it is hoped the colours will be developed. Among the several breeders who are experimenting along these lines are Mr. Frank Reinelt and Dr. A. A. Samuelson. Both have devoted much time to the problem and have achieved a certain amount of success in producing shades of red, orange and pink by crossing *D. cardinale* with various species, but so far they have not succeeded in persuading *D. cardinale* to pass its scarlet colour on to the garden hybrids.

The outstanding personality among the Continental breeders is Mr. B. Ruys, of Dedemsvaart, Holland, whose name will be famous in delphinium history as the raiser of *D. Ruysii* Pink Sensation. For many years Mr. Ruys had endeavoured to cross-fertilize *D. nudicaule* with *elatum* delphiniums, but without any success. Eventually in a batch of seedlings of the red species *D. nudicaule* a purple coloured plant was discovered which appeared to be a hybrid between *D. nudicaule* and an *elatum* type delphinium. Seed was gathered and eventually by constant selection *D. Ruysii* Pink Sensation was developed. The reason for Mr. Ruys' failure to effect the hybridization by hand pollination was because *D. nudicaule* has two sets of eight chromosomes, and the *elatum* hybrids have four sets of eight chromosomes, which makes seed development very difficult. What apparently happened to the parent of Pink Sensation was an accidental doubling of the chromosomes

I. Mrs. Frank Bishop

in *D. nudicaule*. Probably the plant of *D. nudicaule* in question had a reduced ovule with two sets, instead of a single set of chromosomes, and this was fertilized accidentally by pollen from an *elatum* hybrid which normally has two sets of chromosomes. Thus fertilization was made possible, and resulted in a hybrid with four sets of chromosomes.

During the years following the close of the First World War, on account of the wonderful progress made in their development, delphiniums became firmly established in public favour, and the flower that fifty years earlier was more or less obscure was now regarded as the Monarch of border plants. Specialists realized that the time was ripe for launching a Society which would take an active part in the further development of this genus ; so on September 27th, 1928, a number of amateur and professional delphinium enthusiasts met and decided to form a Society, which was to be known as " The British Delphinium Society." The first exhibition of the B.D.S. (as it is called for short) was held on July 5th, 1929, in the Royal Horticultural Society's hall in Vincent Square. The results exceeded all expectations and the future of the Society was assured. Shows were held every following year with increasing success until the War put an end to that part of the Society's activities in 1939. In June, 1946, the B.D.S. resumed its exhibitions with a show that was on the whole a very creditable performance considering the depleted condition of every one's garden, but it must be admitted it was not up to the very high standard of the pre-war years.

The advancement of the delphinium to the important position it now occupies in horticulture is due in no small measure to the interest taken in it by the Royal Horticultural Society itself. In 1932 a Joint Committee was formed, composed of an equal number of members of the R.H.S. and the B.D.S., with a R.H.S. chairman. The committee's charter was to grant Awards of Merit to deserving varieties, and to recommend that those they considered worthy should be sent to Wisley for trial, where varieties that prove themselves to be specially suitable for garden purposes are also honoured with an Award of Merit.

CHAPTER II

PREPARATION OF THE SOIL

*

DELPHINIUMS are universally regarded as the Monarch of border-plants, but I think this term is only applicable to well-grown specimens of good varieties. Then they are truly regal.

They are not difficult plants to grow. Any garden with heavy or light soil in which the usual run of hardy plants are happy will be satisfactory for them, but land of a peaty nature is not recommended as they have a very definite aversion to acid conditions. The preparation of the ground is possibly the most important point in their culture, and the measure of success will be governed by the thoroughness with which this is carried out.

All gardeners are not in agreement about the depth the soil should be dug and the type of manure that should be incorporated into it. There are those who advocate trench-ing 3 ft. deep ; while at the other extreme are some who denounce deep digging, pinning their faith on shallow cultivation combined with surface manuring. With regard to manures, some advocate the use of so-called artificial manures in conjunction with organic manure, and others maintain that artificial manures are responsible for all the plant diseases and troubles that plague a gardener. Since the preparation of the soil is such an important operation in all branches of gardening, before deciding to dig 2 or 3 ft. deep, as the case may be, it is advisable to examine the why and wherefore of digging in its relation to plant nutrition, and not grope about in the dark, hoping the best course is being followed.

Plants obtain their food from the soil in liquid form by means of minute root hairs which are mainly situated near the root tips in great numbers. The plant nutrients are in solution in the film of moisture that surrounds each particle of soil, and the root hairs on making contact with the moisture, absorb the food contained therein into the plant. Therefore two things are obvious :

1. The organic manure that is incorporated into the soil must be broken down and become liquid before a plant can assimilate any nutriment from it ;

2. A continuous supply of moisture is essential.

Organic manure is the term applied to animal excreta, to all parts of dead animals such as bones, hair and flesh, and to dead plants, which when decomposed becomes food for living plants. There are various agencies in the soil which are concerned in breaking down organic matter until it ultimately becomes humus. The principal of these are bacteria and worms.

Worms play an important part in this breaking down process. Organic material together with soil passes through their bodies, and after the worms have extracted the nutriment they need, the residue is discharged upon the surface of the soil in the form of worm casts. Darwin estimated that worm casts amount to as much as 14 to 18 tons per acre per annum. In effect this means that worms bring to the surface of the land a layer of 1 to 1½ ins. of rich soil every 10 years.

With regard to soil bacteria, the subject is too complex and scientific to deal with at any length in a book of this description. Briefly, soil bacteria are extremely small unicellular organisms that inhabit the soil in countless millions. They feed upon organic matter in the soil, turning it into plant food, and extract nitrogen from the atmosphere, making it available to plants. They are absolutely essential to plant life, so particular care must be given, when preparing the soil, to supply their needs. Fortunately, there is no difficulty about this as the majority of plants require similar conditions. These are :

1. An adequate water supply,

2. Soil that is not in a very acid condition.

Worms also dislike an acid soil. When land is found to be deficient of worms it is fairly certain that lime is needed.

The question of soil acidity is a very important one. We have seen that bacteria and worms will not tolerate a very acid soil. Neither will delphiniums, nor will most other plants for that matter. Acidity also has a great effect upon some plant foods. In acid soils phosphoric acid becomes less available, and aluminium and iron become available in too large quantities for the well being of the plants ; on the other hand, when the soil is alkaline, some of those elements such as boron, copper, iron, manganese and zinc, which are essential to plants in minute quantities, are quite unavailable. Therefore, to make sure that the delphiniums will thrive, every care should be taken when preparing the soil to provide conditions in accordance with their needs.

The measurement of soil acidity is expressed by the symbol pH. It is a chemical as well as a mathematical symbol that indicates the degree of acidity. When the pH is 7·0 the condition is neutral, that is neither acid, nor alkaline. Most plants, including delphiniums, are best suited by a slightly acid soil round about pH 6·0 to 6·5. The following is a table of pH values :

Very strongly acid	pH 4·5 to 5·0
Strongly acid	pH 5·0 to 5·5
Medium acid	pH 5·5 to 6·0
Slightly acid	pH 6·0 to 6·5

Neutral	pH 6·5 to 7·0
Slightly alkaline	pH 7·0 to 8·0
Strongly alkaline	pH 8·0 to 9·0

Soil acidity is corrected by dressing the ground with hydrated lime, or finely ground lime stone. When the land is excessively acid a heavy application is necessary, sometimes as much as 2 lbs. per square yard being required to raise the pH up to 6·0 or 6·5, but great care must be exercised not to apply lime in excess, which would make the soil alkaline, a condition unsuitable for most plants and very difficult to correct.

It is impossible to offer general advice about the quantity of lime to apply as land varies so much in its requirements, even in the same district. Any one knowing his ground to be very acid should send a sample to an advisory chemist for advice about the quantity of lime needed to correct the acidity. However, if border plants flourish in your garden and worms are abundant there is no need to worry about the soil condition, but where lime has not been applied during the past three or four years, a dressing of 4 ozs. per square yard would be beneficial in most cases. Gardens where lime hating plants thrive, such as Rhododendrons and Ericas, will undoubtedly need a more or less heavy dressing of lime before delphiniums can be expected to flourish.

Delphiniums are thirsty subjects, therefore it is particularly important during their growing season that they should not lack water. In the early months of the year this is usually supplied in adequate quantity by rainfall, but with the arrival of the hot dry days of Summer, when the plants' need is greatest, their life would be short if rainfall were the only natural supply. Far down below the surface of the ground, at varying depths, is a water supply which keeps up a steady flow of the vital fluid to the surface by means of capillary attraction, but this flow of water from the water-table to the plants can be, and sometimes is, interrupted by unfavourable conditions—conditions that unthinking gardeners unwittingly create themselves.

For water to ascend by capillary attraction there must be a continuous column of firm soil down to the water table. When trenches are dug and thick sandwiches of manure are dumped in the bottom a break is made in the soil continuity, and the water supply from below is blanketed off. It will remain so until the manure decomposes and the soil continuity is again established. The same thing happens in loose soil. The contact, particle to particle, is broken, and until the soil settles down again into close contact the flow of moisture by capillary attraction is badly hampered, or completely cut off, and the plants, if the weather is hot and dry, may suffer from lack of moisture.

An illustration of the effect of capillary attraction can be observed on a piece of freshly dug land in dry weather. The loose surface of the soil quickly dried, but walk across the surface and in a short time the footprints will become damp, showing that the loose soil has been pressed into firm contact with the soil below, and capillary attraction, which had been interrupted by digging, is again in operation in the footprints.

Now let us view the situation regarding the organic manure that is to be incorporated into the ground. The principal nutrients needed by delphiniums (and other plants) are nitrates, phosphates, and potash, labelled for short N.P.K.—N. for Nitrates, P. for phosphates, and K. for potash. These are contained in varying quantities in compost, farmyard, and other organic manures, and are gradually released into the soil as the manure decomposes. When complete decomposition has taken place there remains a black mould-like residue known as humus. The great value of this humus is its capacity for holding moisture. For this reason sandy soils, which are naturally dry, are greatly benefited by a good supply of organic manure.

Regarding the use of manures, there are two schools of

thought. One school maintains that the N.P.K., plus the humus added to the soil by dressings of organic manures, supply plants with all the nutrients they need for their well-being. The second school holds that it is better to supplement organic manuring with chemical fertilizers to augment any deficiencies of N.P.K., according to the special needs of the various plants being cultivated. This is a practice I have always followed and I firmly believe it to be the best.

We have seen that plants only take up nutrients in liquid form. Consequently, all organic manures must decompose before the N.P.K. content becomes available as plant food. Therefore, it is obvious that it is not advisable to dig into the ground large quantities of fresh farmyard or other organic manure. It is far better to procure the manure a few months before it is to be used and compost it together with all the garden refuse available, so that by the time digging operations commence the heap of organic manure is in a well-rotted condition.

Without the slightest doubt deep cultivation is essential for growing good delphiniums ; this, however, does not mean digging 3 or 4 ft. deep—two spits are ample, but there are cases when it is not advisable to dig even as deep as this. Where there is only one spit, or less, of good soil, and the subsoil is of an unkind nature such as solid clay or chalk, then it is best to concentrate on making the top soil as rich as possible, and break up the subsoil by forking into it leaves, garden refuse, cinders, and such material that would keep the soil open and assist drainage.

Since the feeding roots of delphiniums are concentrated mainly in the top spit, many of them being just beneath the surface, it is a mistake to take out a deep trench and dump all the manure in the bottom. When manure is placed deep down in the soil it is out of reach of the principal feeding roots, and as it decomposes the nutrients are washed out of the soil without the plants receiving any, or very little benefit from it. But manure, thoroughly mixed with the

II. A variety of florets

soil from top to bottom, is closely intermingled with the feeding roots and they absorb the food as it is released from the decaying matter.

The next point to consider is the actual digging operation. Assuming that a plot of vacant ground is being prepared and that there are 12 to 18 ins. of good top soil, it is best to begin by taking out with a spade a trench 2 ft. wide and one spit deep, and to wheel the soil to the end of the plot where the digging is to terminate. Then put in the trench a layer of the coarsest manure some 3 or 4 ins. deep and fork it into the second spit, mixing it thoroughly with the soil. Next fill in the trench with the adjacent 2 ft. of top spit, adding manure in the process and mixing it thoroughly with the soil right up to the surface. The value of composting the manure will now be appreciated ; in its half-rotten condition it is short, and is easily mixed with the soil, but fresh, long, strawy manure is more difficult to handle. Continue forking manure into the bottom of each trench and filling in the top spit as before, right to the end of the plot, where the last operation will be completed with the soil deposited there from the first trench. In addition to the organic manure, 8 ozs. of fine bone-meal per square yard should be incorporated into the top spit, and finally a dressing of hydrated lime, or finely ground lime stone, should be spread evenly over the surfaces and raked in, the quantity to apply being according to the needs of the soil.

No hard and fast rule can be laid down about the amount of manure to apply since soil varies so much in its requirements, but very good delphiniums can be grown on reasonably fertile soil with an application of about one cubic yard of manure to every 100 square yards of ground. There is, however, no need for despair if this quantity is not available. When only a small amount is to hand, concentrate it in the top spit where the feeding roots can avail themselves of all the nutrients it contains, and supplement it with artificial manures applied in liquid form about the beginning of May when the plants are in full growth and the bloom spikes are just forming in the heart of the shoots.

Digging operations should be completed, if possible, two or three months before planting so that the soil can settle down into the firm condition necessary for successful plant growing.

CHAPTER III

GENERAL CULTIVATION

*

THE successful cultivation of delphiniums is mainly a matter of doing the right thing at the right time in the right way. The fine flowers exhibited at shows are not produced by growers who have any special knowledge that is unknown to others, neither have they any secret fertilizer " up their sleeves," as many people imagine. They are keen growers who, understanding the needs of their plants, at the right time carry out the many necessary cultural operations in the best possible manner. That is the whole secret of their success.

Planting

It cannot be laid down as a hard and fast rule that any particular time of the year is best for planting, because it depends upon the type of plant with which one has to deal. Plants purchased from a nursery need different treatment from cuttings struck in one's own frame. When dealing with purchased plants extra care is needed. Much of the soil has been shaken from their roots before they were packed, then they have been transported by train and generally a few days have elapsed between lifting and replanting, which is a check to the plants. Careful planting, however, followed by a thorough watering will bring them safely through. Should the weather be very hot some light shading from direct sunshine will help them to recover. If it is not possible to obtain the plants before the middle of September then it is better to defer planting until the Spring, because there is a danger of losing those planted in the Autumn, especially on heavy soils. The best time for Spring planting depends mainly upon the weather. When the shoots begin to push through the soil the sooner they are planted out the better. In mild winters it is sometimes possible to plant in February, but severe weather may make it necessary to delay the operation until March or April.

Cuttings struck in the early months of the year should be well rooted and hardened off by the end of April and ready for planting out into their flowering quarters in May. They will bloom in the late Summer and Autumn and provide flowers of the finest quality the following year. This is unquestionably the best method, and the one that intending exhibitors should practise. A few weeks after the cuttings are planted out, small bloom spikes will develop, these should be pinched off as soon as they appear so as to encourage new shoots to break at the base. One or two of these new shoots may be allowed to bloom in the late Summer and Autumn, but any beyond this number should be cut off at the ground level.

In cases where suitable positions in the border are not available for planting in May, the rooted cuttings must be transplanted, as soon as possible, from the frame to temporary quarters, when they will remain until old and obsolete plants are dug up after flowering to make way for the new ones. The final planting may take place any time from July until early September, and here let me add the earlier the better. It is not really advisable to plant as late as the end of September, but it can be carried out successfully if the plants are carefully lifted with a large ball of soil so that there is a minimum of root disturbance.

The correct method when planting is to make a hole considerably larger than the plant, set the plant with the crown about 1 in. below the surface, fill in around the roots with fine soil, and with a spade chop down the walls of the hole so that the ground surrounding the plants can be firmly pressed down with the feet. A thorough watering should then be given.

3. *The British Delphinium Society's Trials at Wisle*

4. A display of present day varieties. Reading from left : Eva Gover, Emily Poynter, Blue Lagoon, Father Thomas, Audrey Mott, Eclipse, Lulu Sanders, Monica Brown

With July and August planting more than ordinary care must be taken to see that the plants have sufficient water, for the ground at this season of the year is usually very dry. Therefore, a day or so before planting, thoroughly soak the soil, and when the plants are in, give another heavy watering, and continue to water them during the hot dry weather as frequently as is necessary to keep the soil moist.

Distances to Plant

The space that should be allowed for each delphinium depends somewhat upon the effect desired as well as upon the size of the border. For large borders devoted entirely to delphiniums the plan adopted at the R.H.S. Wisley trials is admirable. They are planted in groups of three plants of each variety arranged in a triangle with 2 ft. between each plant. The triangles are arranged in staggered rows down the border with sufficient space, which should not be less than 3 ft., to walk between the triangles. The effect is very impressive.

In large herbaceous borders groups of delphiniums are more effective than single plants, but in small borders the lack of space makes group-planting impracticable and single plants frequently have to be used. In any case no other plants should be placed within 2 ft. of delphiniums. When they are grown in borders by themselves, as they frequently are by exhibitors, they can be planted in single rows $1\frac{1}{2}$ to 2 ft. from plant to plant with a path not less than 3 ft. between the rows, or in double rows 2 ft. apart with a 3 ft. path between the double rows. The sizes given are an absolute minimum, more space should be allowed when possible.

Thinning

With the lengthening days of the New Year, delphinium shoots will begin to break through the soil, sometimes in the South as early as the end of January, but more often about the middle of February. In the Midlands and North the season is generally ten days, or a fortnight later. The first shoots to appear are usually the strongest and these should be selected to remain on the plants for flowering spikes, leaving one or two more than will be finally required, as accidents frequently happen to young shoots, and it is wise to have shoots in reserve, which can be thinned later on.

If cuttings are required, the next best shoots should be taken for striking and the remainder cut off close to the ground. It is a great mistake not to thin delphiniums ; when all the shoots are permitted to flower, sometimes a dozen or more, only very poor spikes are produced and the results are certain to be disappointing. As a rule only one shoot should be left to bloom the first year unless the plant is very vigorous when two can be allowed, but in subsequent years the plants will carry four or five spikes of fine quality.

Hoeing

With some authorities hoeing, as a means of conserving moisture in the soil, has fallen into disrepute, but I still believe it is beneficial to keep a loose surface around the plants. Even if it fails to conserve moisture, it certainly keeps weeds in check. So frequent hoeing is recommended, but care must be taken not to hoe too deeply as delphinium roots are very near the surface. I always like to run a " dutch " hoe through the soil a day after watering, since the loose tilth created is much better than a hard surface when the plants are being watered or fed with liquid manure, the hoed ground holds the liquid while it soaks into the soil, whereas much of it would run off hard soil and the plants would fail to benefit.

Staking and Tying

Following thinning the next operation is staking. Few things are so offensive to the eye as ugly stakes and badly tied plants, so every effort should be made to stake and tie delphiniums neatly, using materials that are as inconspicuous as possible. I now use $\frac{1}{4}$ in. galvanized steel rods instead of canes and find them very satisfactory. They are very pliable, swaying in the wind without damage to the plants. Other points in their favour are their permanence, and they are less conspicuous than any other kind of stake. At present they are almost unobtainable, but in the future I think they will take the place of bamboo canes.

Long bamboo canes, when used for tall varieties, are somewhat unsightly until the spikes are sufficiently developed to hide them. A better plan is to use 5 ft. canes $\frac{5}{8}$ in. thick, which will stand about 4 ft. out of the ground. When the flower spikes begin to lengthen, very thin bamboo canes, known as " carnation tips," are inserted into the top of the canes. " Carnation tips " are 4 ft. long, tapering from about $\frac{1}{8}$ in. up to a knitting needle point, and are strong and whippy. When putting the 5 ft. canes into the ground care should be taken that there is an open hole at the top to receive the " carnation tip." The holes and tips vary in size and a tip can always be found to fit. The combined height of the two canes is about 8 ft., which is sufficient to accommodate any variety. The bloom spikes, as they grow, are loosely looped with green twist to the thin canes right up to the tip, and generally come safely through any wind short of a gale. I have used this method for exhibition blooms for many years and can thoroughly recommend it.

As a rule it is best to supply a stake to each stem, but plants with four, or more, stems can be made secure by using three stakes in a triangle, but in this case tie each spike separately to a stake and do not just pass a string round the three stakes. Such a method may be satisfactory for other plants, but with delphiniums each individual shoot must be tied if damage by winds is to be avoided. It is wise to stake the plants while they are still small and not delay until they are running up to bloom. The best time is from the beginning to the middle of April when the plants are about 9 to 12 ins. high. The stakes should be pushed some 9 ins. into the ground and about 6 ins. away from the stems, and should incline slightly outwards.

The best materials for tying are greentwist, which is inconspicuous, or soft fillis string. The ties should be looped in a single circle round the cane and stem and not tied first round the cane and then round the stem. The lower ties, where the stem becomes very stout, should be made with sufficient tension to support the stem, but higher up among the flowers the ties must be quite loose, allowing a certain amount of sway to the spike, otherwise it will not stand up to the wind but would snap off at the uppermost tie. Occasionally, for additional support, it will be found necessary to tie some of the stems to two stakes in different directions. Frequently old ties have to be readjusted as the spikes grow in order to hold the flowers away from stakes that would damage them.

When the flower spikes begin to lengthen, and until they attain almost their full length, they are very sappy and brittle and during hot weather will sometimes twist and curl in all directions. Any attempt to restrain them by tying in these cases may end in disaster, but by the time the lower florets are ready to open the spikes will have stiffened and generally straightened. Loose ties can then be made, one near the bottom flowers, one in the middle and another near the top of the spike to safeguard it from being broken by strong winds.

Mulching and Feeding

Although a number of enthusiasts grow delphiniums for exhibiting, they are few compared with the many thousands who grow them for the wonderful effect they make in their gardens in association with other plants. Many plant them in mixed borders without any special soil preparation and are quite satisfied with the relatively poor spikes that result, not realizing how much finer the flowers would be if only

III. Delphinium Pink Sensation

IV. Delphiniums under glass at Baker's Boningale Nursery

a little effort were made to provide them with the nutriment they need for their well-being. Any one not acquainted with well-grown delphiniums would be amazed to see how much finer and more beautiful they are when good treatment is provided. Unless the ground has been deeply dug and manured feeding is of little avail, but in conjunction with well-prepared soil, liquid manure will add considerably to the length and breadth of the spikes, size of the florets, and general beauty of the flowers. A mulch of compost, farm-yard, stable, or hop manure, while not being essential, is of great benefit to the plants. Whenever it rains, or they are watered, the roots receive nutriment from the mulch. It also conserves moisture in the soil. The best time to apply it is during April before the ground begins to dry out. It should be spread 2 or 3 ins. thick for 2 ft. all round the plants.

At the beginning of May, when the plants are 12 to 18 ins. high, is the time to commence feeding with liquid fertilizer. Although as yet invisible the bloom buds are just beginning to grow in the heart of the shoots, and the liquid manure will have a great effect in developing the spikes to their full capacity. The feeding should be continued at fortnightly intervals until the bottom florets show colour, when it should be discontinued.

A complete fertilizer such as " National Growmore," or any similar fertilizer that has a good percentage of potash, should be used. The following can easily be made up by those who prefer to prepare their own mixture. Super-phosphate of Lime 2 parts, Sulphate of Potash 1 part, Sulphate of Ammonia, or Nitro Chalk, 1 part (by weight). The first feed should be on the weak side, ½ oz. per gallon of water is sufficient, giving each plant 2 gallons, and applying it for 18 inches all round the plants. Later on, when the plants are more fully developed, the amount can be increased to ¾ oz. per gallon of water, but no stronger solution than this is advisable. In cases where it is not convenient to apply the fertilizer in liquid form it can be sprinkled around the plants at the rate of 1 oz. per plant, taking care to keep it off the foliage and well away from the stems. When rain is expected apply the fertilizer in time for the rain to wash it in, but during a dry period a hose-pipe or watering can must be used, giving each plant two or three gallons of water to carry the nutriment well down to the roots. Feeding should not be carried out when the soil is very dry. When this is the case the plants should be well watered the previous day.

Watering

Of the many things necessary for the well-being of delphiniums none is more important than water. No matter how well the ground has been prepared, nor how fine and strong are the plants, if an ample supply of water is not available during their growing period they will not thrive. Unless therefore Nature supplies it in the form of rain resort must be made to the hose-pipe or watering-can. Moreover, it is not sufficient to sprinkle a few cans of water around the plants moistening only the surface of the soil. When the soil becomes dry during a rainless period in the summer three or four gallons per plant are needed to soak the ground down to the full extent of the root run.

For some years past I have had under observation the effect of water on delphiniums and have arrived at the conclusion that probably more delphiniums die from lack of water than from any other cause. In situations where the soil is naturally moist delphiniums frequently live for many years, but in dry soils their life is often of short duration. A critical time is the period following their blooming when they are frequently neglected, because so few people trouble to water them after they have flowered. July and August are generally the hottest and driest months of the year, and the plants, more or less exhausted with flowering, are so badly affected by the lack of water that many die during the Autumn, and others become so weak that they fail to survive the winter. Black rot is usually blamed for the losses, but in my opinion dryness at the roots is at the bottom of the trouble. Following the severe drought in August, September and October of 1947, an unusual number of delphiniums died, which is further evidence in support of this theory.

Treatment after Flowering

There is a difference of opinion among delphinium growers about the best method of treating delphiniums after they have flowered in June and July. Whether it is better to force them into a second crop of flowers or to discourage them is a controversial point on which strong arguments can be made in favour of either method. My personal opinion is that it depends upon the purpose for which they are grown. I would restrain from second flowering, as far as possible, plants being grown for show blooms :

1. By not cutting down the main spikes after they had flowered, leaving them to die down naturally at the end of the summer.

2. By leaving a few seed pods to ripen on the spikes.

3. By keeping the plants somewhat on the dry side, but of course not dry enough for the plants to suffer.

These measures would have a restraining influence on the dormant eyes, the plumpest of which are needed for next season's exhibition flowers. But no matter how one tries to restrain them, some shoots will break up from the base and flower later in the summer. They will not break as freely however as those that receive the following treatment which I recommend for garden plants.

When delphiniums are grown for garden adornment, as the great majority are, it is most desirable to have them in flower for a long period, and everything possible should be done to extend their flowering season to the utmost, provided always it is not detrimental to the plants. Therefore, instead of trying to restrain them, as advised for exhibition plants, the delphiniums in the border can be stimulated into new growth by treating them in the following manner.

In July, when the main spikes have shed their florets, cut out the faded part of the spikes, leaving the lateral blooms to carry on the display, and as these fade they should be removed. This is the time when so many delphiniums are neglected ; they have finished flowering and no further interest is taken in them. If instead of this neglect, which frequently results in their death from want of water, the plants are thoroughly watered and fed, a very different result is achieved. The blank spaces are again filled with a new display of flowers, and although not as fine as those of the early Summer, they are particularly welcome since they supply the lovely blue shades that are so scarce in August and September border flowers. When the laterals have been removed the plants should be thoroughly watered. This should be followed a day or two later by a feed of liquid manure similar to that given to the plants in May, applied at the rate of 1 oz. in two gallons of water per plant ; and ten days later a similar watering and feeding should be given. The effect of this will be that new shoots will break into growth at the base. When these are growing strongly cut the old stems down to within 6 ins. from the ground, and thin out the new ones, leaving, say, two of the strongest shoots. These will bloom in late August and September. After they have flowered they should not be cut down, but should be left to die down in the late Autumn. If the spikes are cut down immediately after flowering it would tend to force them into flowering a third time, which would be detrimental to the plants, for only weak eyes would be left for flowering the following year. This treatment will keep the plants active until they die down in the late Autumn with a healthy root system to carry them through the winter.

With the arrival of winter the plants will become dormant. The stakes should then be pulled up and stored, and the plants cleaned up by removing all the foliage and cutting the stems down to about 6 ins. from the ground. Hoe around the plants and clear away all weeds and rubbish that would make a hiding place for slugs. If coarse sharp sand or rough sifted cinders (not ashes) are available, place a covering over the crown of the plants to make it uncomfortable for slugs, who delight so much to hibernate in delphinium crowns and devour the dormant eyes. Examine the labels and see that they are sound and the names legible. If any plants have died, now is the time to prepare the ground for the new ones that will take their place in the spring.

The work for the year is now completed and there is nothing further to be done until the plants break into growth ready for propagation in the early Spring.

CHAPTER IV

PROPAGATION

★

O F the countless thousands of people who cultivate a flower-garden most of them, sooner or later, find the need for increasing their stock of plants. Many hardy border flowers are propagated by dividing old plants, but, in the case of delphiniums, this is not the best practice. Some people dig up their old delphiniums, chop them into small pieces and replant them. A serious objection to this method is that should there be any disease in the old crown, as there frequently is, the disease is passed on to the new plants.

The three methods of increasing delphiniums, in general practice, are by :

1. Seed
2. Cuttings
3. Division or splits

Seed

If we divide our plants or take cuttings we get varieties of exactly the same kind as the plant from which they were taken. This, however, is not the case with seed. Since delphiniums are the product of cross-fertilization, seedlings are seldom exactly like the plant from which the seed was gathered. This is one of the reasons why growing delphiniums from seed is so fascinating ; there always seems a chance that something new and good may turn up among the seedlings. Breeding will be dealt with more fully in a later chapter ; here we are only considering seed purchased from a nurseryman, or gathered from one's own plants. Those who grow the best named varieties can save a few seeds on them and rely on obtaining a proportion of good seedlings, but unless they are first-class modern varieties the seed is not worth growing.

In the case of purchased seed, I cannot too strongly urge that it should be obtained from delphinium specialists. These firms have stocks of the finest varieties in commerce from which they obtain their seed ; they also are continually breeding new varieties and obtaining the latest novelties of other raisers, seed from which, in due course, is included in their seed packets.

There is no great difficulty in raising delphiniums from seed, but, in common with most things, there is a right and a wrong way of doing it. Failures are not uncommon, chiefly because insufficient care is given to a few important details. Some of the things that affect germination are : unsuitable compost ; sowing too deeply ; temperature too high or too low ; insufficient or excess of moisture ; and lastly, exposure to direct sunlight. More seedlings are lost through the misuse of the watering-can than from any other cause. It is vital to keep the soil moist while seed is germinating, for once the soil becomes dry there is little hope of the seed surviving ; but the secret is to keep it " moist " and not " wet."

A point to remember when sowing seed is that soil is not easily moistened when it is quite dry. Be sure then that the compost used for seed sowing is in a moist condition, otherwise when the seed is sown and the box is watered with a fine rose watering-can, the surface of the soil will be wet, but the soil beneath may be quite dry, the water having drained down the side of the box without penetrating the soil. Compost for seed sowing is tested for moisture by taking a handful and squeezing it tightly in the hand. Its condition is correct if it retains its shape but crumbles into loose soil when pressed by the fingers. Should it not retain its shape when squeezed it is too dry, and if it will not crumble it is too wet.

An efficient method of watering seed-boxes and pots is to immerse them in a tank of water, but not deep enough to allow the water to overflow into the box. The water will find its way through the drainage holes and gradually percolate through the soil and flood the surface. This does not disturb the seed as watering with a can often does, and the soil is thoroughly moistened. Probably no further watering will be needed before the seed germinates, provided the box is covered with a piece of glass to prevent evaporation. A sheet of paper should be placed over the glass to exclude light, since seed germinates better in the dark.

The use of unsuitable compost is a frequent cause of bad germination. The term " compost " may be confusing to the uninitiated, since there are two distinct kinds of compost in gardening. When loam, sand, peat and other ingredients are mixed in varying quantities for potting and seed sowing, the result is known as " potting and seed compost," and the heap of garden refuse which used to be burnt, and now, because farmyard manure is scarce, is rotted down into organic manure by every good gardener, is also called " compost." Here, of course, I refer to the former.

It is a common practice with some people to take soil from their gardens and, without any preparation, use it for seed sowing. They may be lucky and bring their seedlings through without mishap, but those who follow this course must not be surprised if none, or only a small percentage germinates. The best results can only be expected when suitable compost and proper conditions are supplied.

Nothing better than the " John Innes " compost can be recommended for seed sowing. It consists of 2 parts sterilized loam, 1 part granulated peat, 1 part coarse sharp sand (measured by bulk), with the addition of $1\frac{1}{2}$ ozs. superphosphate of lime, and $\frac{3}{4}$ oz. ground limestone, per bushel of

V. *L to R* : Harrow, Marjorie Bradshaw, Mayflower

compost. The compost can be purchased mixed ready for use from many nurserymen, or can be mixed by any one having the necessary ingredients.

As a general rule owners of heated greenhouses have little difficulty in raising seedlings. Delphiniums seed can be sown towards the end of January, or in February, in a greenhouse with bottom heat. These seedlings will bloom in the late Summer of the same year, and make grand plants the following season. The temperature of the house should not fall much lower than 40° F. at night, while 60° F. in the daytime is ample.

A greenhouse, however, should not be used for raising delphiniums from seed in the Summer. Greenhouse temperatures in the summer months are often far too high for the seed to germinate, since 60° F. is the ideal temperature and above 80° F. will be fatal. The better course during hot weather is to stand the seed-boxes in a cool airy room or shed, no matter how dark until the first seedlings are through the soil. Then they must be moved immediately into a light, but shady position with plenty of air, and kept out of direct sunlight for a week or two, and, what is most important, they must be kept moist.

There is no better time for sowing seed than the latter half of July, as soon as it is harvested. This being nature's time for sowing one cannot do better than follow her example, but sowing at this season of the year should not be delayed much later than the middle of August, since the seedlings from later sowings would be too small to transplant in the Autumn and would have to remain in the seed-boxes until the following Spring. This freshly gathered seed is full of vitality and upwards of 80 per cent can be expected to germinate.

Delphinium seed does not keep for a very long time, in fact it loses its vitality rather quickly. Seed that would germinate up to 100 per cent when it is gathered, may drop to 50 per cent by the following Spring, and to less than

25 per cent by the Summer. It will, however, keep in perfect condition for a year or two if stored in air-tight jars in a refrigerator at a temperature of 36° F. to 40° F.

Since the seedlings raised in July are generally too small to be planted into the open ground in the Autumn, they should be pricked out, about 2 ins. apart, into seed-boxes as soon as they are large enough to handle and wintered in a cold frame. They may then be planted out into the garden during April, when the weather conditions are favourable, in the place where they will flower during August and September. It is the modern practice to prick out seedlings while they are very small, and not wait until their second, rough leaves have developed. By this method there is less damage to the roots and the seedlings make better progress. Seed not sown by the end of August should be kept until the following Spring, and sown any time from April until July. Later the seedlings should be pricked out into frames or boxes, and when large enough planted out into the garden. Blooms must not be expected the same year, but fine plants will be made and they will flower the following June.

If the quantity of seed to be sown is small, say up to 100, it is best sown in a 4½ in. flower pot, but seed-boxes about 15″×9″×3″ deep are better for a larger number. Crocks should be placed in the bottom of pot or box for drainage before filling them with seed compost. This latter should be pressed down firmly with a piece of flat wood, and the seed sown thinly on top. The seed should then be very lightly covered with finely sifted soil, care being taken not to bury the seed too deeply since this is a frequent cause of poor germination. A good general rule for sowing seed is to cover it with soil to a little more than the depth of its own thickness. After covering, again firm the soil with the piece of wood and water the box by immersion in a tank of water. Finally cover it with a sheet of glass with paper on top. In warm conditions germination may commence in about nine days, so a careful watch must be kept for the first seedlings to appear. The paper and glass should then be removed and the seedlings brought into a light but shady position out of doors. Seed may be sown in the open ground from April onwards, but good delphinium seed is expensive and slugs are particularly fond of seedlings. Unless precautions are taken against these pests it is not worth running the risk of losing all when the danger can be avoided by sowing in boxes.

Raising delphiniums from seed is an easy way of providing a large number of plants at little cost, but people must not delude themselves with the idea that seedlings are just as good as the best named varieties. Even in the finest strains of seed only an occasional seedling is up to that standard.

Cuttings

It is only by growing the finest named varieties that the infinite charm and beauty of delphiniums can be appreciated. Those who introduce these aristocrats of the border into their gardens are seldom satisfied for long with having only one plant of a variety. Where borders are large groups of three or more are far more effective than single plants, and more than one group of a favourite variety is often desired. Therefore to increase the stock propagation by cuttings or division must be carried out.

Most delphinium specialists propagate by cuttings, although division, known as " splitting," is to a certain extent practised. This, when properly carried out, is satisfactory, but unquestionably cuttings are superior to splits. These cuttings are not difficult to strike, but to be successful certain conditions must be observed. The cutting must be severed right at the point where it joins the crown of the plant, for here the stem of the cutting is solid. A short distance from the crown the stem becomes hollow, and if cut there failure is certain. Even if it should root a crown would not form.

FIG. 1.

Nurserymen as a rule lift their delphiniums for propagating, but most amateurs take their cuttings from plants growing in borders. They are taken as soon as the shoots come through the ground and are 3 or 4 ins. high. This may be any time from early February until April, the time varying according to the season; moreover some varieties commence growth much later than others. The most vigorous shoots should be left on the plants to supply

5. An exhibition spike. D. Cynthia Bishop. Note well-formed spike and evenly-spaced florets

6. Plants cut down for winter, and surrounded by sifted cinders as a protection against slugs

7. (*Below*) Planting. Showing depth to plant and how to firm soil round roots

blooms during the coming season, and
the cuttings should be selected from the
next best shoots. But on no account should
thin and weak growths be used.

The soil should be scraped away from
the crown of the plant with a wooden
label so that the junction of the shoot
with the crown is clearly seen. Care must
be taken not to damage the roots which
are very near the surface. Then with a
sharp knife sever the cutting close against
the crown of the plant (Fig. 1). The base
of the cutting should be neatly trimmed,
any damaged edges being removed and
all the lower leaves and loose pieces of
husk cut off close to the stem (Fig. 2).

For amateurs the best method is to
strike the cuttings in a cold frame. If a
frame is not available, a temporary one

FIG. 2.

may be constructed easily with four pieces of 9 in. board and
some loose sheets of glass to cover the top. The frame
should be made of a size to accommodate the number of
cuttings required. About 2 dozen cuttings can be struck
in every square foot of frame. I have struck many thousands
of cuttings in this type of frame with complete success.
My frames were 6 ft. long by 2 ft. wide. Some were covered
with loose sheets of glass and others with " Windolite "
nailed on wooden frames. Where only a few plants are
required a box 9 ins. deep can be adapted for the purpose
by removing the bottom, and covering the top with loose
glass. Since there is a danger of the glass being blown off
in windy weather a clip should be fitted as a safeguard.

The frame should be placed on the garden, preferably in
a sheltered spot, where the soil is reasonably good. A
dressing of sharp coarse sand should be forked into the top
6 ins. to keep it open, and the soil firmed by pressing

it down with a board. A thin covering of coarse sand should then be spread over the surface and the cuttings dibbled in 1 in. deep. Press them in firmly, in rows 3 in. apart with 2 in. between the cuttings. Thoroughly water and cover with lights or sheets of glass. It is important to keep the frame tightly closed so as to exclude as much air as possible until the cuttings are well rooted, which usually takes four or five weeks. While not essential it is advisable to lime-wash the glass to shade the cuttings from the sun. To exclude frost, on very cold nights, the frames should be covered with sacking. After the initial watering further watering may not be needed for two or three weeks, especially with early cuttings ; but with later ones the warmer and sunny days of April may make more frequent watering necessary. However, it is vital to keep them moist, since dry soil will kill them outright.

As soon as the cuttings are rooted they will begin to grow, the lights should then be tilted slightly to admit a little air. This should be gradually increased day by day, until finally, in favourable weather, the lights should be removed altogether to harden off the cuttings before planting out in early May. Where space is available they can be planted at once into their permanent positions in the border, otherwise they must be transplanted 9 ins. apart into temporary beds where they can remain until the border is ready to receive them. When lifting them from the cutting frame keep as much soil on the roots as possible to prevent a serious check to their growth and above all see that they do not suffer from lack of water.

A large number of cuttings are struck by trade specialists in heated greenhouses. It is a good method for amateurs to follow if a suitable greenhouse is available, but unless care is taken to provide proper conditions the result may be very disappointing. A close atmosphere is needed for the cuttings to strike, but it must not be too humid, otherwise they will rot. They will not tolerate the moist atmosphere of a propagator.

If this method is to be adopted the stools should be lifted about the beginning of January and replanted close together in boxes with the soil just covering the crowns. They should then be stood on a bench in a heated greenhouse, or they may be laid in close together in trenches in a border of the greenhouse. The heat must be sufficient to keep frost out at night. In a very short time the shoots will begin to grow, and as soon as they are 2 or 3 ins. high the plants should be taken from the box, or trench, and the cuttings that are large enough removed. All weak shoots should be rejected. If there are any strong eyes still dormant, the crowns should be replanted for a second crop of cuttings.

The best method for striking is to pot each cutting separately in a 3 in. pot in " John Innes seed compost," giving the cuttings a good watering and standing them on ashes on a bench in the greenhouse. All the ventilators should be closed until the cuttings are rooted. The temperature should be kept up to 40° F. at night, and during the day 60° F. is sufficient. Success largely depends upon careful watering. Do not over water, but on no account allow them to become dry. The morning is the best time for watering since moisture on the foliage then quickly evaporates, whereas watering late in the day may result in the foliage remaining wet all night, and the cuttings in consequence are liable to rot. When the cuttings are rooted, air should be admitted to the greenhouse, and as soon as weather conditions are favourable they should be transferred to a cold frame and hardened off ready for planting.

Division

Finally, there is propagation by divisions. Dividing an old delphinium crown by cutting it into pieces with several shoots in each division is a most unsatisfactory method. The crown of an old delphinium is invariably decayed and frequently disease is present. To cut this into pieces and

Fig. 3.

replant them is inviting trouble. Strong healthy plants cannot be expected by this method, but when a strong single shoot with roots attached, known as a split (Fig. 3), is cut from an old plant and every part of the crown that is decayed is cut away, leaving only healthy tissue, then a good plant will probably result. All the thick thong roots should be cut away leaving only the fibrous ones which should be shortened to about 2 ins. in length. The divisions can then be planted straightway into the border. There is, however, not the slightest doubt that a cutting taken as described formerly provides a better, healthier and more satisfactory plant from every point of view.

CHAPTER V

DISEASES AND PESTS

*

ALTHOUGH delphiniums, in common with other plants, have their particular enemies and diseases, none of the diseases to which they are prone in this country is deadly enough to cause growers very deep concern. It is true that many succumb to the disease known as " black rot," but up to the present time all the investigations that have been made have failed to establish definitely if it really is a disease or only a secondary effect caused by unhealthly conditions, or unsuitable treatment.

The symptoms of the disease are a yellowing of the foliage, followed by the collapse of the plant. By lifting the plant it will be discovered that the upper roots, the crown and stem of the plant have rotted into a black jelly-like mass of decay. Frequently all the roots are blackened and dying, but sometimes the lower roots seem to be healthy, which suggests that the decay works downwards.

Mr. D. E. Green, the eminent mycologist at the R.H.S. Gardens, Wisley, conducted considerable research on " black rot " during the years preceding the war. His conclusion was that the disease is not due to a fungus parasite ; and, that, although there is a possibility of the disease being of bacterial origin, he thought it to be un-likely. He writes : " We are more probably dealing with an unhealthy condition brought about by some adverse condition, or set of conditions, in the cultivation of the plant. In such case the weakened roots and crown would be more easily invaded and rotted by various organisms naturally present in the soil, especially bacteria—these being secondary to the original cause of the trouble. They can thus be isolated from affected roots, but fail to cause the disease when inoculated back into vigorous roots."

The opinion held by some growers is that " black rot " is caused by water entering the crowns by means of the hollow stems left on the stools, thus setting up conditions that would encourage rotting organisms. Others consider that the use of chemical fertilizers is to blame. Experiments to test this were conducted at Wisley between 1934 and 1936. The results showed that there was no appreciable difference in the mortality among plants where no fertilizer was applied and others where sulphate of ammonia, sulphate of potash, superphosphate of lime, and a complete fertilizer were used. The disease is far more prevalent among plants propagated by division than those grown from cuttings. Where cuttings have developed the disease it will probably be found that the cuttings have been taken from diseased plants previously propagated by division. The danger of propagating from such plants can easily be observed if the shoots of a diseased plant are examined. Many of them will be found with blackened tissue inside the base of the cutting. Such shoots should never be used for cuttings as infected plants are certain to result.

My own convictions on the causes of " black rot " are based on observations, and not on scientific investigation. Before the war I kept delphinium plants only for one year. As soon as they had flowered they were dug up and replaced by new ones raised from cuttings. But in 1943, owing to other demands on my time, I was obliged to alter my method and had to leave the old plants in the ground to flower a second and third season. The result of this was that I came up against the problem of delphiniums dying during the Autumn and Winter, presumably from " black rot." During the autumn of that year, in a batch of 200 plants, over 25 per cent died. I had not experienced such a tragedy before and was mystified why plants, that were in the best of health when they were flowering in July, should suddenly contract this disease and die in the short space of two or three months. On lifting the dead plants I found that the roots and crowns had all rotted away. A careful consideration of the problem convinced me that want of water was the only possible cause. July, August and September of that year were exceptionally dry, little rain had fallen during the whole period. The plants, which had been well watered and fed up to the time of their blooming, were for three months without moisture. Consequently their vitality was so seriously affected that they were unable to resist the attack of the disease organisms which prey on unhealthy plants. I concluded that the rotting of the crowns and roots was really a secondary effect and that the primary cause of their decease was the want of water.

With these convictions in my mind I decided to carry out an experiment the following year (1944) with a larger batch of plants. The rainfall in the spring and summer of that year was very small and, in consequence, the ground in early July was very dry and badly cracked, in spite of the heavy waterings the plants had been given in May and June. Early in July, as soon as the flowers had faded, the spikes were cut off, leaving the foliage intact. The plants were then given a very thorough watering, followed a day later by an application of " Growmore " fertilizer in liquid form. A week later the watering and feeding were repeated. The effect was to start the basal buds into growth. As soon as the new shoots were growing strongly they were thinned to two, and the old stems were cut down to the ground. My object was to encourage the plants to make vigorous new growth and to flower a second time in the late summer. By this means when the foliage died down in the winter the plants would have developed a healthy root system full of vigour, instead of being half-dead from want of water. The plants, which were fed three times in all and were thoroughly watered at frequent intervals, responded wonderfully to the treatment. During the late summer they provided a fine show of spikes, almost as good as those in June. In the winter only six plants out of 400 died, an enormous improvement on the previous year, although the weather, as far as rain was concerned, was very similar in both years.

Here a word of warning is needed about the danger of forcing plants into bloom again *after* the second crop. If this is done the result is weak plants and poor spikes the following year. To discourage any further autumn flowering, a few pods of seed should be allowed to ripen on the second spikes, watering and feeding should be discontinued, and all the foliage be left on the plants to die down naturally.

In support of my contention that abundant moisture is necessary to keep delphiniums healthy, further evidence is supplied by the following account of a friend's experience over a period of nine years.

His garden consists of heavy loam with a subsoil of solid clay and is situated at the lowest point of a building estate. All the surrounding land drains down to his garden and there is no possibility of the garden being drained to get rid of the surplus water. The result is that his garden is never dry, even in the driest summer the soil is always moist. In winter the garden remains very wet, and during a rainy period it becomes flooded. It is sometimes completely submerged for weeks up to a depth of 6 ins. In this garden he grows exceptionally good delphiniums, so good that in 1938 he won the Lord Riddell Memorial Cup at the British Delphinium Society's Show and was second in the same class in 1937. But the astonishing thing is the length of time his delphiniums live in these apparently unsuitable boggy conditions. The plant, Sir Neville Pearson, which produced the Cup winning spike in 1938, was still alive in 1946 ; and a spike from the same plant won the medal for the best spike in the show at the 1946 B.D.S. exhibition, the plant at this time being nine years old. Moreover, it was not a case of only one plant living for many years. In 1946, all the fifty delphiniums in his garden were old plants, none less than five years old, ten were seven years and fourteen were eight years old. To me the significant point is that, owing to the low lying position of his garden, his delphiniums were never dry at the roots, and this, I think, is the reason for their longevity. But this story has a sequel, and it is sad to relate that the exceptional severity of the seven weeks frost in January, February and March in 1947, followed by the floods in the Thames Valley, when his garden was deep under water for weeks, has caused the death of all his delphiniums.

Another disease that attacks delphiniums is known as " black spot," and is caused by *Bacterium Delphini*. An attack may be recognised by unsightly black blotches which form on the leaves. Some varieties are more prone to it than others, but except for the ugly spots and blotches which disfigure the leaves and sometimes spread to the stems, there is nothing to worry very much about in this disease. It does not result in the death nor any very serious damage to the plants. There is no known method by which " black spot " or " black rot " may be controlled.

Mildew, a parasitic fungus called *Erysiphe Polygoni*, is another disease to which delphiniums in this country are susceptible. While not being a deadly complaint, it is very unsightly and causes a great deal of injury to the foliage and stems. This weakens the plants and impairs their vigour, resulting in poorer plants the following year than would have been the case had their foliage been healthy. Some varieties are much more prone to attack than others, and a few are resistant. The disease seldom makes an appearance before early July, but once it starts, and if the weather conditions are favourable it will spread rapidly. As long as the weather is dry and the atmosphere is not humid there is little danger of it, but with the appearance of moist, muggy weather such as we get when thunderstorms are about mildew will soon be found on the most susceptible varieties. Unless measures are taken to control the disease it will spread quickly to all but the resistant varieties. It flourishes among crowded plants where the free movement of air is impeded.

With mildew, as with most other diseases, prevention is better than cure, and a spraying with lime sulphur, commencing the first week in July before any plants are actually attacked, and repeated at fortnightly intervals, would help to keep the disease in check. A 1 in 60 solution of lime sulphur is a good spray for the purpose. It can also be controlled by green sulphur, which should be applied by means of a powder sprayer.

In common with most other kinds of plants, delphiniums are sometimes attacked by virus diseases. Most growers at one time or another may have observed their plants with distorted blooms and foliage, and may not have realised that in all probability the plants were infected with a virus disease. Of the several virus diseases that attack delphiniums in various parts of the world, particularly in America, *Cucumis Virus I*, known as " Cucumber Mosaic Virus," is the only one that we in the British Isles need to worry about at present. It is fairly common in English gardens, and, since the disease is incurable, growers should acquaint themselves with the symptoms of the disease and destroy every infected plant.

The characteristic symptoms are—a distortion of the foliage and sometimes the flowers. The leaves of affected plants frequently present a chlorotic appearance and are more or less distorted. The segments of the leaves are narrow and elongated and the tips of the segments become very long and sharply pointed. The leaves may also have pale green areas following the veins and a green mosaic mottle. Distortion of the flowers is not always present, but sometimes the florets are much reduced in size and have a distorted, withered appearance as shown in the illustration on Plate 12. The colour and substance of the sepals are also affected. " Cucumber Mosaic Virus " attacks over 100 different kinds of plants and is carried from plant to plant by aphides, but since delphiniums are rarely infested by aphides they are not so liable to the virus infection as most other plants. However, once a delphinium is infected it is incurable, and every cutting and division of the infected plant will carry the virus.

Of the various pests that attack delphiniums, slugs are the worst, and every effort must be made to exterminate them. In gardens where they are prevalent, unless measures are taken to reduce their numbers and to safeguard the crowns against their attacks, they will devour the young shoots, and sometimes completely ruin the plants.

There are two distinct methods of dealing with these pests. The first is to protect the plants against their attacks, the second, to attack the slugs. I am a believer in attack being the best form of defence, and am convinced it is so when fighting slugs. Since they produce many hundreds of eggs each season, obviously, it is a better policy to kill them than to concentrate on protecting the plants, but, no doubt, a combination of the two methods is the best plan to follow. The plants can be protected, to some extent, in their dormant season by removing the loose soil from their crowns when they have died down in the autumn, and covering them with coarse, sharp sand, or rough sifted coke cinders, so that the crowns are made too uncomfortable for the slugs to use as winter quarters. It is quite common to find most of the dormant eyes, in an unprotected crown, devoured by slugs. Another protective measure is to encircle each plant with a narrow band of zinc, since slugs will not travel over zinc. But before placing the bands around the plants, care must be taken to see that no slugs are left enclosed within the bands.

Useful as these protective measures are, it is far better to wage war on slugs throughout the garden with the various chemical preparations now obtainable. Kill as many as possible, and so protect not only the delphiniums but also all the other plants which attract them.

Of the various killers used in the destruction of these slimy pests, one that can be employed with unfailing success is " Meta " (now known as Metaldehyde), a solid form of methylated spirit, and which has an irresistible attraction for slugs and snails. The " Meta," which is sold in small bars, should be crushed into a fine powder and thoroughly mixed with slightly moistened bran, using 6 bars of " Meta " to 1 lb of bran. The mixture should be placed in small heaps of about a teaspoonful, about a foot apart among the plants, and in wet weather it is best covered by a piece of slate or wood to prevent it being washed into the ground. The following morning quantities of the slugs will be found lying around the bait dead or in a dying condition.

" Anti-slug " is an alum preparation that I have used with great success. It not only kills all the slugs with which it comes into contact on the surface of the soil, but also destroys their eggs in the ground, and further prevents their breeding in the area treated for a considerable time. It is obtainable in powder form and is best applied by means of a sprinkler. A tin, with small holes perforated in the lid, makes an efficient sprinkler for the purpose.

Another equally successful method is to poison them with " Paris green," a form of arsenic which must be used with care. 1 oz. of " Paris green " should be thoroughly mixed with 1 lb. of moistened bran and scattered very thinly over the ground. This should only be used in dry weather as rain would wash it into the soil.

Another remedy little known is " Paradichlorobenzine," which can be procured from any chemist. The crystals should be crushed almost to a powder. Then holes 3 ins. deep and about 1 yd. apart should be made with a " dibber," and a saltspoonful of the crushed crystals put in each hole, and the hole closed up. It is claimed that the fumes, which can be detected when digging the ground months later and which are harmless to plants, will kill most, if not all of the slugs in the treated ground.

In addition to those mentioned, there are many other preparations on the market that can be relied upon to carry death to the loathsome invaders. I have little faith in the old-fashioned method of dusting soot and lime around the plants. They are not very effective, and after every shower of rain fresh applications are needed. Also, the use of orange skins, cabbage leaves and such things, under which slugs will hide in daylight involves spending valuable time each day in collecting and destroying the catch. All these things are out of date, and are superseded by more efficient modern methods of chemical warfare.

Other pests that do a certain amount of damage to delphiniums are wireworms, cutworms and leather jackets. The last two do harm principally to young seedlings, cutworms—by eating them off at the ground level—and leatherjackets—by attacking them beneath the soil. The " Paris green " bait, already described, is the best method of destroying them. Wireworms are a more difficult problem. They do a considerable amount of damage by boring through and through the crowns. It is not uncommon when lifting old crowns to find them infested with wireworms. The best way to combat this pest is to dress the ground with a soil fumigant such as " Naptholine " or " Vaporite."

Finally, there are the caterpillars that make a nest in the top of the shoots in May and June, and eat the bloom spike that is just beginning to form. It is particularly annoying to an exhibitor to find the heart eaten out of a stem that promised to provide a fine show spike. It pays exhibitors to make a daily inspection during May and June, of the bloom spikes that are just making an appearance. The presence of caterpillars can be detected by the gumming together of the small leaves in the centre of the shoots, and all that is needed to put an end to their existence is the gentle pressure of a finger and thumb.

Possibly it is not wise to focus the attention of readers too much on these diseases and pests, for it is easy to get a distorted view of their seriousness. There is nothing in them to deter any one from taking up the culture of delphiniums. In fact, by comparison with many other plants, delphiniums are very healthy ; and provided they are given reasonably good cultivation and are not neglected, particularly in regard to watering, there is no reason why they cannot be kept as healthy as any other plant in the border.

CHAPTER VI

A REVIEW OF
MODERN VARIETIES

*

DURING the present century delphiniums have probably made greater strides than any other plant. Every characteristic of the flower has been improved, not only are the spikes longer and heavier, but the individual florets are larger and are better formed. Moreover the range of colour has been considerably enlarged especially in the pure blue section.

In conjunction with this the single and double varieties have rather lost favour and the semi-doubles form is now firmly established as the popular type. Some twenty years ago, before the semi-double self blues were firmly established, there was a great demand for single blue varieties such as Mrs. Townley Parker. But breeders during recent years have succeeded in developing semi-double self blues which are comparable with the best mauve varieties, and as a consequence singles have, to a large extent, lost their popularity. A few, however, are still worthy of a place in any garden, the best perhaps being Mrs. Townley Parker, a pale blue early flowering variety, Blue Beauty and Wrexham Glory, charming mid-blues ; but possibly the most attractive of all, because of its fine spikes and exquisite mixed colouring of pale blue and pale mauve, is Wild Wales.

Double delphiniums, which are mostly of the "ranunculus" type, are not very popular. The reason for this is probably because they lack the attractive contrast the " eye " gives to the semi-doubles. The best of the double varieties are Alice Artindale, a blue and mauve variety which possesses a better spike than most others; Codsall Lad, dark blue and purple; and Glory of Wales, a blue and mauve which is especially valuable because it flowers very late in the season. Lady Eleanor is often regarded as a double, but it is, in fact, a semi-double, its waved inner petals giving it the double effect; but whether it is considered a semi-double or a double, it is well worth a place in every garden.

But it is on the semi-doubles that we will concentrate because, without a doubt, they are the most attractive and important of those grown to-day. One of their chief charms is the variety of their floret formation; another, the build of their spikes. Moreover they have a wide range of colour which extends through every shade of blue, violet, mauve and purple and even includes white and cream.

Together with the singles a further attractive feature in the semi-doubles is the " corolla," a small cluster of petals in the centre of the floret, which is known as the " eye." This " eye " varies considerably in different varieties. In some it is as large as a shilling, in others it is quite insignificant, whilst in a few cases it is absent altogether. The colour of the " eye " is one of its attractive features, and this ranges from white to cream and yellow and all shades of brown to black. Some are self-coloured, others have stripes of blue and mauve. Whether a black " eye " is more attractive than a white or brown is a matter of personal preference, but a point on which every one agrees is that the " eye," large or small, must be neat and must not straggle over the floret.

In reviewing the delphiniums, which leading experts of to-day regard as the cream of present-day varieties, it is sad that we have to ignore many lovely plants that have given so much pleasure in past years. But as with everything else, varieties which were in the front rank ten or fifteen years ago are now superseded by newcomers who possess better form, brighter colours and improved habits. Some veterans, however, still hold their own, such as Lady

8. D. *Belladonna* Blue Dragonfly

9. A Himalayan species.
(D. *Brunonianum*)

10. Seedlings grown from seed stored in a refrigerator for 12 months. Normally few delphinium seeds as old as this would germinate

Eleanor and Sir Neville Pearson to mention but two, and they have been in the forefront for the best part of twenty years and are still unsurpassed in their particular type and colour. A good way, perhaps, to assess the real value of a variety is by the number of years it continues to be grown and loved by critical gardeners. I say " critical gardeners " advisedly because so many members of the general gardening public retain old varieties long after their useful purpose has been served and they have been superseded by much finer delphiniums. So long as an old variety bears tolerable comparison with the modern ones there is no reason why it should be dropped out of cultivation, but when it is definitely superseded, then the sooner it is discarded and forgotten the better, sad though it may be to do so.

By kind permission of the British Delphinium Society their register of varieties is reproduced at the end of this chapter. This register consists of varieties that have received Awards of Merit, and, in the opinion of the Delphinium Joint Committee, are the best in cultivation. Each year this register is reviewed and brought up to date by deleting those varieties which have been superseded, and adding new ones that gain honours during the current year. Recently this register has been made all the more useful as the varieties have been grouped broadly in colour sections, thus helping members in their selection. But it must not be thought for a moment that varieties listed in any one of the colour groups are necessarily alike. Most of them are quite different from each other. For instance, in the pale blue and pale mauve section you will find Lady Eleanor, Nora Ferguson and Wild Wales grouped together, but three varieties more unlike can not be imagined. Why, then, you may ask, are they included in the same section ? The reason is that the colour combination of each is pale blue and pale mauve.

The written word cannot convey any real idea of the beauty of the Delphinium and it would only be a waste

T.D.   E of time endeavouring to describe the charm of form and colour of the older varieties which are already known to the public. There are, however, a number of new ones that have only become available during the last few years. Few people are at present acquainted with them. I, therefore, propose to give some notes on these novelties. In addition, mention will be made of a few noteworthy varieties that are too recent to be included in the register, therefore an alphabetical list has been added as an appendix. Among these are some of the newest raised by Messrs. Blackmore and Langdon and Messrs. Hewitts. I am much indebted to Mr. Alan Langdon and Mr. George Phillips for supplying a brief description of their novelties, and as I am unacquainted with many of them I cannot enlarge upon their various merits.

PALE MAUVE

There are no novelties in this section.

MAUVE

In the mauve group are two novelties—Blackmore's Glorious and Brigadier F. E. Hotblack. Although among the older varieties there are some fine varieties that have been popular for many years, the newcomers, when well-known, will rival them in public favour.

Blackmore's Glorious is a fine delphinium. The light mauve and blue florets centred with a large white eye are well formed and of the largest size, measuring $3\frac{1}{2}$ to 4 ins. in diameter. They are openly spaced on pyramidal spikes of gigantic proportions. It is a vigorous grower and is resistant to mildew. As an exhibition variety it will take a prominent place.

Brigadier F. E. Hotblack. I remember being much attracted to this variety when it was put up for Award. The florets are uncommon in form, the sepals being longer and more pointed than usual. Its colour is an attractive shade of clear pinkish mauve shaded blue, the eye is black and very prominent. The florets are evenly spaced on well-built spikes.

Boningale Glory. (Not in the Register.) Medium mauve and pale blue. An exceptionally tall variety with a spike of bloom of 5 ft. A fine exhibition variety.

DEEP MAUVE

The three varieties in this section are quite distinct from each other both in colour and build. All are good delphiniums, the only novelty being—W. R. Chaplin.

W. R. Chaplin. A rich shade of deep mauve, eye black. The fine large florets are evenly spaced on well-built massive spikes of medium length. Easily the best variety in this section for exhibitors.

VIOLET PURPLE

Among the older varieties in this group " Sir Neville Pearson " is supreme. It has had a long run of popularity and is still in the front rank.

The new varieties are Brutus and Father Thames and several that are not in the Register namely Cynthia Bishop, Chopin, Leonard Petrie, Michael Blackmore, Nigger and Startling.

Brutus. A rich shade of dark blue and plum purple, and a black and gold eye. The florets are very large and are evenly spaced on good spikes. Its excellent habit makes it a first-class border plant.

Father Thames. An exceptionally healthy, robust and free-flowering variety. The rosy violet and gentian blue florets are somewhat closely spaced on good spikes of medium length. A fine garden plant, mildew resistant.

Cynthia Bishop. This is probably the richest violet self-coloured delphinium in commerce. The large well-formed florets have the lustre and texture of violet velvet. Good pyramidal spikes.

Chopin. Methyl violet suffused Bishop's violet, pure white eye. Early flowering.

Leonard Petrie. A most striking variety. The very deep violet self-coloured florets with a white eye are borne on very stiff well-built spikes.

Michael Blackmore. Deep violet purple with a small black eye, the florets are somewhat closely spaced on broad pyramidal spikes. One the earliest varieties to bloom. The colour is almost unique in the garden.

Nigger. A very deep violet self, practically without an eye. A very strong grower.

Startling. Another rich deep violet variety with a prominent eye, startling in its effect as its name suggests.

PURPLE

The only purple novelty is Beau Nash. Of the older varieties Lady Amy is unique in colour, but a more robust plant with the same rich colour would be welcomed. Lady Teresa when well-grown is a good exhibition flower. Lord Derby is a veteran that has deserved its long run of popularity.

Beau Nash. I was impressed with this variety at the Wisley Trials. The deep purple and dark mauve florets centred with a black and gold eye are evenly spaced on well-built spikes of exhibition quality. It is a fine garden plant.

DARK BLUE

For years people have been clamouring for blue delphiniums. Breeders have been accused of concentrating upon the mauve colours and neglecting the pure blues. The criticism is unjust because nobody has been more eager to develop the blues than the breeders themselves. The fact is the development of semi-double pure blue has been a very slow process, and it is only in quite recent years that self-coloured semi-double blue delphiniums with large florets and spikes comparable with the best mauve varieties have become an accomplished fact.

At present there are few that can be regarded as selfs among the dark blues, but in the near future many more will become available.

The newcomers in this section are :

Blackmore's Blue, a deep sky-blue self with a white eye. The very large florets are evenly spaced on good tapering spikes. A very choice variety.

Viking. Not a pure blue, but a rich deep blue with rosy purple shading and a sepia eye. Good heavy spikes. Very late flowering.

Harrow (not in the Register), is a variety of outstanding merit and a decided advance in blue delphiniums. The perfectly shaped large florets of cornflower blue deepening towards the edge of the petals, with a neat white eye, are ideally placed on heavy pyramidal spikes. The quality of its blooms combined with its very robust habit places it in the front rank as a garden and show variety.

MID-BLUE

" Delphinium blue " is a term in fairly common use, but no one could define the exact shade of blue the name implies. It is, in fact, a term covering the whole range of mid-blues from sky to gentian blue.

In the mid-blue group some of the most lovely varieties are to be found. Of the twenty listed, many are lightly suffused with shades of rose and pink, some being more heavily flushed than others, but in a few cases the blue is as pure as can be found in any flower. The beauty of these pure blue delphiniums is a joy to behold.

Gremlin and Puck are my own varieties, but as they are not up to the very high standard of present-day blue delphiniums they have been destroyed.

Agnes Brooks and Mrs. Frank Bishop are the novelties in this section, and with the darker blue Harrow they are the forerunners of a strain that will set up a new standard for blue delphiniums. Their florets and spikes are comparable in size and quality with the finest mauve varieties, while for vigour and stamina they are second to none.

Agnes Brooks has enormous florets of pure cornflower blue carried on exceptionally long pedicels, and a striking large white eye splashed blue. The florets are openly spaced on very large spikes.

Mrs. Frank Bishop. The bright gentian blue florets centred with a large black eye are ideally spaced on long tapering spikes. A first-class show and border variety.

Blue Lagoon. Bright gentian blue with a flush of rose-purple, and a neat dark eye. A good garden and exhibition variety.

Ellen Wort. Mid-blue flushed rose, with a white eye. A useful border variety.

Elsie Edwards. Another gentian blue with a rose suffusion, and a brown eye. Somewhat after the type of Blue Lagoon, but a different shade of blue.

Eva Gower. Cornflower blue flushed rose, and a white eye. Good spikes of exhibition quality.

Gwladys Sharpe. Large slightly cupped florets of deep gentian blue flushed purple rose. Eye dark. The florets are rather closely spaced on medium length spikes.

Watkin Samuel. From every point of view this is an outstanding delphinium. Its bright sky-blue self colour makes it every one's favourite. It is vigorous, healthy, mildew resistant, and has a fine heavy spike.

The following varieties are not at present included in the Register.

Sylvia Blackmore. Sky-blue self with a white eye. A very vigorous variety and mildew resistant.

Bath Heights. Clear blue self with a small white eye. The spikes are long and tapering. A tall variety useful for planting at the back of the border. Mildew resistant.

Flora Campbell. Gentian blue with a small white eye. A choice variety with long graceful spikes.

Frederick Grisewood. Gentian blue self with a small white eye. A first-class variety that invariably makes an excellent spike.

Chas. F. Langdon. A lovely medium blue self with a black eye. This variety appealed to me very much when I saw it at the Chelsea Show. The florets are of fine form and are well placed on good spikes. It is a vigorous grower and mildew resistant.

Mayflower. Bright gentian blue, deeper on edge of the petals. White and blue eye. Perfectly formed florets of the largest size. Heavy pyramidal spikes.

Mistress Page. Cornflower blue, paler in centre of floret, small black eye. Large well-shaped florets on massive tapering spikes.

The last two varieties are of the same breed as Harrow and have just the same vigour and excellence of form as that variety.

PALE BLUE

The dainty Cambridge and forget-me-not blue varieties are lovely in mixed flower borders, where their spikes of soft blue are invaluable for associating with pink, salmon and orange colours of other flowers.

Most of the varieties in this section are new, but only a few can be regarded as blue selfs, the majority having a slight flush of pink or rose.

Beryl is not at present on the market.

Eclipse. Cobalt self blue with a small black eye. The thin-stemmed spikes are elegant and well furnished with medium-size florets. Its lovely colour and free flowering habit will make this a favourite border variety.

Etonian. Another pure Cobalt blue variety, but quite distinct from Eclipse, which was one of its parents. The florets are large and well formed with a black eye. It is very useful for positions near the front of the border as it seldom exceeds 4 ft. in height. The broad tapering spikes are rather short and the florets are openly spaced.

Margaret Pratt. Azure blue slightly flushed pink with a small black eye. A good pale blue garden or show variety.

May Docwra. Soft sky blue with a white eye. A good variety with an excellent spike.

Mother of Pearl. A dainty combination of forget-me-not blue with a pink sheen and an amber eye. A spike of moderate proportions with evenly-spaced florets of perfect form.

Sea Nymph. Somewhat near Margaret Pratt in colour but a different type of spike and rather taller habit.

Sylvia Blackmore. Sky-blue self with a white eye. A very vigorous variety and resistant to mildew.

Two newcomers (not included in the Register) are Jill and Harvest Moon.

Harvest Moon. An exquisite pale blue with a prominent black eye. Exceptionally free flowering. A grand garden variety.

Jill. Has attracted attention in the nursery. The inner petals are waved, giving a double effect (after the style of Lady Eleanor). The colour, however, is much bluer than that variety, being a lovely shade of French blue with the faintest flush of pink in the base of the floret. The well-built spikes are moderate in length.

PALE BLUE AND PALE MAUVE

In this colour group blue is the dominating colour, but there is too much mauve in their colouring for them to be classed among the blues.

Lady Eleanor stands pre-eminent in this group of lovely delphiniums, most of which are veterans. If a vote were taken to decide which is the most popular delphinium in cultivation, there is little doubt Lady Eleanor would head the poll.

The novelties are :

Audrey Mott. Outer petals pale sky-blue, inner ones soft rose and sky-blue. Small white eye. Long shapely spikes. First-class show and garden variety and lasts well when cut.

C. H. Middleton. Rich medium blue, suffused pale mauve and a sulphur white eye. The large well-formed florets of good texture are closely spaced on broad pyramidal spikes. A fine garden and exhibition variety.

Jennifer Langdon. Pale blue and mauve with a small black eye. The very large florets are of remarkable substance and exceptional keeping quality. An additional recommendation is its resistance to mildew. Excellent for garden and exhibition.

PALE MAUVE AND PALE BLUE

The varieties in this section generally have blue back sepals, the inner ones being various shades of pale mauve, heliotrope and lavender, sometimes the inner petals have a suffusion of blue.

The only novelty in this group is not in the Register.

Sheba. Lilac mauve splashed sky-blue, eye white. An excellent grower with fine broad spikes.

BLUE AND MAUVE

There is such a wide divergence in the colour of these varieties that it is difficult to believe they all belong to the same section. However, it must be realised that one group merges into another, and border line varieties might correctly be placed in either of the two groups each side of the border line. For example, Monica Brown is on the border line of Pale Blue and Pale Mauve and could have been included in that section. The same thing applies to the darker varieties in this section D.B. Crane and Monarch of Wales. Both of these varieties could have been placed in the Mauve and Blue Section because blue is not the dominating colour in either variety. But as long as it is realized that the colour group is not a colour description, but only a broad colour band in which the varieties are placed, then we shall not be led astray.

Of the varieties listed Lorna Doone, Monica Brown, Emily Wort, Swallow Tail and Darkie are new, but the last three are not at present on the market.

Lorna Doone. Lilac with sky-blue back sepals and a small black eye. It is a vigorous grower and has a well-formed heavy spike.

Monica Brown. French blue flushed rosy mauve, scarcely any eye. An elegant free flowering garden variety.

MAUVE AND BLUE

The two listed varieties are not at present in commerce.

Elizabeth Reckitt has a unique floret. The petals forming the very large eye give an anemone effect. The colour is an unusual shade of purplish mauve backed with gentian blue. The spike is small and the growth not very vigorous.

Princess Alexandra. Medium mauve with a bluish edge and no eye. The fine large florets are rather closely spaced on good long spikes.

Julia Langdon. (Not in the Register.) Mauve, slightly tinged with blue and a white eye. The very large florets are of wonderful substance. The spikes are pyramidal in form and very wide at the base. A grand exhibition variety.

MAUVE AND PALE BLUE

George Bishop is the outstanding variety in this section. The colour is an attractive shade of pale rosy purple backed with cobalt blue and centred with a large brown eye. The very large florets are perfect in form and are carried on fine long spikes of exhibition quality. A good garden variety.

Lulu Sanders. Inner petals heliotrope backed sky-blue and a neat dark eye. The florets are large and the spikes massive. A good show and garden variety.

Sonia Hotblack. Pinkish mauve and forget-me-not blue. (Not in commerce.)

DARK BLUE AND MAUVE

Pyramus. An attractive delphinium, somewhat different in form from the usual run of varieties. The deep blue florets, lightly shaded mauve, are almost eyeless and have several rows of petals in the manner of Lady Eleanor. The fine, broad, tapering spikes are of exhibition quality.

Cantata. Gentian blue heavily suffused Bishop's violet. White eye tipped gentian blue. Well-formed florets and good pyramidal spikes. (Not in the Register.)

DARK BLUE AND PURPLE

There are plenty of light and mid-blue varieties to choose from, but the rich deep blues, which are so effective in the garden are rather scarce.

Sir Joseph Skevington. A most remarkable delphinium that commands attention wherever it is seen. The rich colour combination is almost unique in delphiniums. The sepals are rich blue in the middle deepening to deep aconite violet towards the edges. The white eye stands out in striking contrast to the intense colour of the florets. The fine symmetrical spikes combined with a very robust constitution places it right in the front rank as a garden and exhibition variety.

Minerva. A rich deep violet self with a black and gold eye. A very fine strong growing variety.

Delius. (Not in the Register.) Sepals gentian blue with a slight suffusion of Imperial Purple at the edges. Large white eye flecked gentian blue.

WHITE

(Not in the Register.)

Handel. Paper white self, white eye flushed cream. Early flowering.

A List of Recommended Varieties all

The recommended list comprises varieties which have receive
were recommended as exhibition varieties at the Royal Horticultur
These are grouped in colours, as seen in the Gardens at Wisle
named colour predominating. The varieties are grouped tentative
This list is intended, as a guide, for the use of members, who c

Variety	Type	Eye	Flowering Season
BELLADONNAS—*Pale Blue :*			
BLUE BEES	Single	White	Early
MUSIS SACRUM	Single	White	Early
Pale Blue and Mauve :			
SEMI-PLENA	Semi-double	Brown	Mid
Mid Blue :			
MRS. J. S. BRUNTON	Single	White	Early
ORION	Single	White	Mid
THEODORA	Single	Brown	Mid
Dark Blue and Mauve :			
ISIS	Single	Purplish	Mid
WENDY	Single	White & Blue	Mid
Dark Blue :			
BLUE DRAGONFLY	Single	Mauve	Mid
LAMARTINE	Single	White	Mid
NAPLES	Single	Purplish	Mid
Pink :			
PINK SENSATION	Single	White & Pink	Mid
ELATUM—*Pale Mauve :*			
LADY CLARA	Semi-double	White	Late
Mauve :			
BLACKMORE'S GLORIOUS	Semi-double	Blue & Mauve	Mid
BRIGADIER F. E. HOTBLACK	Semi-double	Black	Mid
CONSTANCE MARMENT	Semi-double	White	Mid
JEAN SMITH	Semi-double	White	Mid
LADY DIANA	Semi-double	White	Mid
LADY GUINEVERE	Semi-double	White	Early
MARGARET FARRAND	Semi-double	White	Late
NELL GWYN	Semi-double	White	Mid
OLIVIA	Semi-double	White	Mid
TESSA	Semi-double	White	Mid

hich have received Awards of Merit

wards at Wisley for garden decoration and those to which awards
ociety's exhibitions in London.
eing graded by the Committee, after many inspections—the first-
nd will be subject to revision in future years.
ot know all the newer varieties.

Height	Awards as Exhibition Varieties	Awards at Wisley Trials as Garden Varieties	Raiser and Introducer
Short	—	A.M. 1935	Bees
Short	—	A.M. 1935	Egmond
Short	—	A.M. 1933	Ruys, Perry
Short	—	A.M. 1925	Ruys
Short	—	A.M. 1937	Koppius
Short	—	A.M. 1933	Carlile
Short	—	A.M. 1933	Gibson
Short	—	A.M. 1941	Carlile
Short	—	A.M. 1946	Mooring
Short	—	A.M. 1935	Ruys
Short	—	A.M. 1935	Wood
Short	—	A.M. 1941	Ruys
Medium	A.M. 1933	A.M. 1935	Blackmore & Langdon
Medium	A.M. 1947	—	Blackmore & Langdon
Medium	A.M. 1942	—	Hotblack
Tall	—	A.M. 1945	Blackmore & Langdon
Medium	—	H.C. 1941	Bees
Tall	—	A.M. 1935	Blackmore & Langdon
Medium	A.M. 1931	A.M. 1935	Blackmore & Langdon
Tall	—	A.M. 1942	Blackmore & Langdon
Medium	—	A.M. 1945	Blackmore & Langdon
Tall	—	A.M. 1942	Blackmore & Langdon
Medium	A.M. 1938	A.M. 1947	Blackmore & Langdon

Variety	Type	Eye	Flowering Season
ELATUM—cont'd—*Deep Mauve :*			
GERALD HOWSE	Semi-double	Black	Late
THE SHAH	Semi-double	Brown	Mid
W. R. CHAPLIN	Semi-double	Black	Mid
Violet-Purple :			
BRUTUS	Semi-double	Brown	Mid
FATHER THAMES	Semi-double	Black	Mid
PURPLE PRINCE	Semi-double	White	Mid
SIR NEVILLE PEARSON	Semi-double	Black	Mid
VIOLET ROBINSON ..	Semi-double	White	Early
Purple :			
BEAU NASH	Semi-double	Brown	Mid
LADY AMY	Semi-double	Black	Mid
LADY TERESA	Semi-double	White & Violet	Mid
LORD DERBY	Semi-double	White	Mid
RANDOLPH	Semi-double	White & Purple	Late
VIOLETTA	Semi-double	Brown	Mid
Dark Blue :			
A. J. MOIR	Semi-double	White	Mid
BLACKMORE'S BLUE ..	Semi-double	White	Mid
BLUE CELESTE	Semi-double	White	Mid
BLUE CAP	Semi-double	White	Mid
DONALD ALLAN	Semi-double	White	Late
DUCHESS OF PORTLAND	Semi-double	White	Mid
F. W. SMITH	Semi-double	White	Mid
LILIAN BISHOP	Semi-double	White	Mid
LORNA	Semi-double	Brown	Late
VALENTIA	Semi-double	White	Late
VIKING	Semi-double	Sepia	Late
WELSH BOY	Semi-double	Brown	Mid
Mid Blue :			
AGNES BROOKS	Semi-double	White	Mid
BLUE BEAUTY	Single	Black	Mid
BLUE BELL	Semi-double	White	Mid
BLUE LAGOON	Semi-double	Brown	Mid
BLUE SPIRE	Semi-double	White	Mid
BLUE STONE	Semi-double	Black	Late
ELLEN WORT	Semi-double	White	Late
ELSIE EDWARDS	Semi-double	Brown	Mid
EVA GOWER	Semi-double	White	Mid
GREMLIN	Semi-double	Blue	Mid
GWLADYS SHARPE ..	Semi-double	Brown	Mid

Height	Awards as Exhibition Varieties	Awards at Wisley Trials as Garden Varieties	Raiser and Introducer
Medium	—	A.M. 1935	Blackmore & Langdon
Medium	A.M. 1942	A.M. 1924	Blackmore & Langdon
Medium	F.C.C. 1946	A.M. 1945	W. R. Chaplin
Medium	—	A.M. 1945	Blackmore & Langdon
Medium	—	A.M. 1945	Bishop, Bakers
Tall	—	A.M. 1942	Blackmore & Langdon
Medium	—	A.M. 1935	Blackmore & Langdon
Medium	A.M. 1931	A.M. 1935	Blackmore & Langdon
Tall	—	A.M. 1945	Blackmore & Langdon
Medium	—	A.M. 1935	Blackmore & Langdon
Tall	A.M. 1931	A.M. 1932	Blackmore & Langdon
Medium	—	A.M. 1925	Blackmore & Langdon
Tall	—	A.M. 1937	Blackmore & Langdon
Medium	A.M. 1939	—	Blackmore & Langdon
Medium	A.M. 1931	A.M. 1935	Blackmore & Langdon
Medium	A.M. 1945	A.M. 1947	Blackmore & Langdon
Tall	—	A.M. 1942	Blackmore & Langdon
Tall	—	A.M. 1942	W. Spencer, Astolat
Medium	—	A.M. 1937	Blackmore & Langdon
Medium	—	A.M. 1937	Blackmore & Langdon
Medium	—	A.M. 1935	Ferguson
Medium	A.M. 1934	A.M. 1935	Bishop, Carlile
Medium	—	A.M. 1941	Blackmore & Langdon
Tall	—	A.M. 1942	Blackmore & Langdon
Medium	—	A.M. 1942	Bishop, Bakers
Tall	A.M. 1932	—	Watkin E. Samuel
Medium	A.M. 1946	—	Bishop, Bakers
Medium	—	A.M. 1935	Watkin E. Samuel
Medium	A.M. 1939	—	Blackmore & Langdon
Medium	A.M. 1945	A.M. 1945	Bishop, Bakers
Tall	—	A.M. 1937	Blackmore & Langdon
Medium	A.M. 1939	—	Marshall
Medium	A.M. 1939	A.M. 1942	Wort, Bakers
Medium	A.M. 1946	—	Bishop, Bakers
Medium	A.M. 1941	A.M. 1945	Bishop, Bakers
Dwarf	—	A.M. 1947	Bishop, Bakers
Medium	A.M. 1941	A.M. 1945	Bishop, Bakers

79

Variety	Type	Eye	Flowering Season
ELATUM—cont'd—*Mid Blue :*			
JUDY	Semi-double	Black	Mid
MRS. FRANK BISHOP ..	Semi-double	Black	Mid
MRS. PAUL NELKE ..	Semi-double	White	Mid
NATALIE	Semi-double	Brown	Late
PHILIP BUTLER	Semi-double	White	Mid
PUCK	Semi-double	Brown	Mid
WATKIN SAMUEL ..	Semi-double	Black	Mid
WHITETHROAT	Semi-double	White	Mid
WREXHAM GLORY ..	Single	Brown	Mid
Pale Blue :			
BERYL	Semi-double	Black	Mid
CRYSTAL	Semi-double	White	Mid
ECLIPSE	Semi-double	Black	Mid
ETONIAN	Semi-double	Black	Mid
LADY HOLT	Semi-double	White	Mid
MAID OF BATH	Semi-double	White	Late
MARGARET PRATT ..	Semi-double	Black	Mid
MAY DOCWRA	Semi-double	White & Blue	Mid
MOTHER OF PEARL ..	Semi-double	Pale Brown	Mid
MRS. TOWNLEY PARKER	Single	White	Early
NAOMI	Semi-double	Black	Mid
OENONE LANG	Semi-double	White	Mid
SEA NYMPH	Semi-double	Black	Mid
SYLVIA BLACKMORE ..	Semi-double	White	Mid
Pale Blue and Pale Mauve			
AUDREY MOTT	Semi-double	White	Late
BRIDESMAID	Semi-double	White & Mauve	Mid
C. H. MIDDLETON ..	Semi-double	Brown	Mid
DAWN	Semi-double	Brown	Late
JENNIFER LANGDON ..	Semi-double	Black	Early
JENNIFER MILLIGAN ..	Semi-double	Black	Late
JILL HOTBLACK	Semi-double	Sepia	Mid
LADY BERTHA	Semi-double	Black	Mid
LADY ELEANOR	Semi-double	White & Mauve	Mid
MRS. T. CARLILE	Semi-double	White	Mid
NORA FERGUSON ..	Semi-double	White	Mid
NORA HOTBLACK ..	Semi-double	White	Mid
ROBINA BICKERTON ..	Semi-double	White	Late
WILD WALES	Single	Black	Mid
Pale Mauve and Pale Blue :			
AYLIFFE	Semi-double	White	Mid
LADY ELIZABETH	Semi-double	Brown	Mid

Height	Awards as Exhibition Varieties	Awards at Wisley Trials as Garden Varieties	Raiser and Introducer
Medium	—	H.C. 1942	Perkin
Medium	—	—	Bishop, Bakers
Medium	A.M. 1929	—	Blackmore & Langdon
Tall	—	A.M. 1941	Blackmore & Langdon
Medium	—	A.M. 1933	Blackmore & Langdon
Dwarf	—	A.M. 1945	Bishop, Bakers
Medium	A.M. 1946	—	Watkin Samuel, Bakers
Medium	—	A.M. 1933	Hill, Carlile
Medium	A.M. 1934	A.M. 1946	Watkin E. Samuel
Medium	—	A.M. 1942	H. A. Perkin
Tall	A.M. 1939	A.M. 1942	Blackmore & Langdon
Tall	—	F.C.C. 1946	Bishop, Bakers
Dwarf	—	A.M. 1942	Bishop, Bakers
Tall	A.M. 1931	A.M. 1945	Blackmore & Langdon
Tall	—	A.M. 1937	Blackmore & Langdon
Medium	—	A.M. 1942	Bishop, Bakers
Medium	—	A.M. 1942	Blackmore & Langdon
Medium	A.M. 1946	A.M. 1945	Bishop, Bakers
Medium	—	A.M. 1933	Blackmore & Langdon
Medium	—	A.M. 1942	Blackmore & Langdon
Medium	A.M. 1937	—	Lang, Bees
Medium	A.M. 1941	—	Bishop, Bakers
Medium	A.M. 1946	—	Blackmore & Langdon
Medium	A.M. 1942	A.M. 1942	Bishop, Bakers
Tall	—	A.M. 1945	Blackmore & Langdon
Medium	—	A.M. 1945	Blackmore & Langdon
Medium	A.M. 1929	A.M. 1933	Spencer
Medium	A.M. 1946	—	Blackmore & Langdon
Medium	A.M. 1947	—	Rickett
Tall	—	A.M. 1942	Hotblack
Medium	—	A.M. 1935	Blackmore & Langdon
Tall	A.M. 1931	F.C.C. 1935	Blackmore & Langdon
Medium	—	H.C. 1947	Carlile
Tall	—	A.M. 1933	Ferguson
Medium	A.M. 1933	—	Hotblack
Dwarf	—	A.M. 1942	Docwra
Medium	—	A.M. 1935	Watkin E. Samuel
Medium	A.M. 1933	—	Lang, Jackman
Medium	F.C.C. 1929	—	Blackmore & Langdon

Variety	Type	Eye	Flowering Season
ELATUM—continued			
Pale Mauve and Pale Blue :			
LADY KATHLEEN ..	Semi-double	White & Mauve	Late
LADY MAY	Semi-double	White	Mid
MRS. HARGREAVES ..	Semi-double	White	Mid
MRS. NEWTON LEES ..	Semi-double	White	Early
ROBBIE	Semi-double	Black & Mauve	Late
VISCOUNTESS HARCOURT	Semi-double	White	Mid
Blue and Mauve :			
ALICE ARTINDALE ..	Double	—	Mid
BLUE GOWN	Semi-double	Black	Early
D. B. CRANE	Semi-double	White	Mid
DARKIE	Semi-double	Black	Mid
EMILY WORT	Semi-double	White	Mid
GLORY OF WALES ..	Double	—	Late
ITALIA	Semi-double	White	Mid
LORNA DOONE	Semi-double	Brown	Mid
MILLICENT BLACKMORE	Semi-double	Black	Late
MONARCH OF WALES ..	Semi-double	White	Late
MONICA BROWN	Semi-double	Brown	Mid
OMEGA	Semi-double	Brown	Late
SWALLOW TAIL	Semi-double	White	Mid
Mauve and Blue :			
ELIZABETH RICKETT ..	Semi-double	Brown	Mid
PRINCESS ALEXANDRA	Semi-double	White	Mid
Mauve and Pale Blue :			
CAMBRIA	Semi-double	Black	Late
GEORGE BISHOP	Semi-double	Sepia	Late
LADY DOROTHY	Semi-double	Black	Mid
LAURA FAIRBROTHER ..	Semi-double	White	Late
LULU SANDERS	Semi-double	Black	Mid
PERCY GODFREY	Semi-double	Amber	Mid
SONIA HOTBLACK ..	Semi-double	Brown	Mid
Dark Blue and Mauve :			
PHILIP BUTLER	Semi-double	White	Mid
PYRAMUS	Semi-double	White	Mid
W. B. CRANFIELD	Semi-double	White	Mid
WYN MARTIN	Semi-double	Blackish-purple	Mid
Dark Blue and Purple :			
CODSALL LAD	Double	—	Mid
MAVIS	Semi-double	White	Mid
MINERVA	Semi-double	White	Mid
SIR JOSEPH SKEVINGTON	Semi-double	White	Mid

Height	Awards as Exhibition Varieties	Awards at Wisley Trials at Garden Varieties	Raiser and Introducer
Tall	—	A.M. 1935	Blackmore & Langdon
Medium	A.M. 1931	—	Blackmore & Langdon
Medium	F.C.C. 1929	A.M. 1937	Bones
Medium	A.M. 1931	F.C.C. 1935	Blackmore & Langdon
Medium	—	A.M. 1935	Blackmore & Langdon
Medium	—	A.M. 1941	Blackmore & Langdon
Medium	A.M. 1936	A.M. 1945	Artindale
Tall	A.M. 1932	F.C.C. 1935	Blackmore & Langdon
Medium	A.M. 1931	A.M. 1933	Blackmore & Langdon
Medium	A.M. 1939	A.M. 1946	Marshall
Medium	—	A.M. 1935	Wort, Bakers
Medium	—	H.C. 1945	Watkin E. Samuel
Tall	F.C.C. 1942	—	Blackmore & Langdon
Medium	A.M. 1942	—	Bishop, Bakers
Medium	—	A.M. 1925	Blackmore & Langdon
Tall	—	A.M. 1928	Watkin E. Samuel
Medium	—	A.M. 1935	Bishop, Bakers
Medium	—	A.M. 1935	Blackmore & Langdon
Tall	—	A.M. 1942	Perkin
Medium	—	A.M. 1937	Rickett
Medium	—	A.M. 1945	Blackmore & Langdon
Medium	—	A.M. 1929	Watkin E. Samuel
Medium	A.M. 1942	A.M. 1942	Bishop, Bakers
Medium	—	A.M. 1926	Blackmore & Langdon
Tall	—	A.M. 1935	Blackmore & Langdon
Medium	A.M. 1941	A.M. 1942	Bishop, Bakers
Tall	A.M. 1939	H.C. 1937	Bishop, Bakers
Medium	—	A.M. 1946	Hotblack
Medium	A.M. 1933	—	Blackmore & Langdon
Medium	A.M. 1945	—	Blackmore & Langdon
Tall	A.M. 1934	—	Blackmore & Langdon
Medium	—	A.M. 1942	Lang
Medium	A.M. 1935	—	Watkin E. Samuel
Medium	A.M. 1942	—	Blackmore & Langdon
Medium	A.M. 1945	—	Blackmore & Langdon
Medium	—	A.M. 1945	Bishop, Bakers

Variety	Type	Eye	Flowering Season	Height	Raiser and Introducer
BATH HEIGHTS	Semi-double	White	Mid	Tall	Blackmore & Langdon
BONINGALE GLORY	Semi-double	Brown	Mid	Tall	Watkin E. Samuel, Bakers
CANTATA	Semi-double	White	Mid	Medium	Wootton, Hewitt
CHOPIN	Semi-double	White	Mid	Medium	Wootton, Hewitt
CHAS. F. LANGDON	Semi-double	Black	Mid	Medium	Blackmore & Langdon
DELIUS	Semi-double	White	Mid	Medium	Wootton, Hewitt
FLORA CAMPBELL	Semi-double	White	Late	Medium	Blackmore & Langdon
FREDERICK GRISEWOOD	Semi-double	White	Mid	Medium	Blackmore & Langdon
HANDEL	Semi-double	White	Early	Medium	Wootton, Hewitt
HARROW	Semi-double	White	Mid	Medium	Bishop, Bakers
HARVEST MOON	Semi-double	Black	Mid	Medium	Bishop, Bakers
JILL	Semi-double	White	Mid	Medium	Bishop, Bakers
JULIA LANGDON	Semi-double	White	Mid	Medium	Blackmore & Langdon
LEONARD PETRIE	Semi-double	White	Mid	Medium	Blackmore & Langdon
MAY DOGWRA	Semi-double	White	Mid	Medium	Blackmore & Langdon
MAYFLOWER	Semi-double	White	Mid	Medium	Bishop, Bakers
MICHAEL BLACKMORE	Semi-double	Black	Early	Medium	Blackmore & Langdon
MISTRESS PAGE	Semi-double	Black	Mid	Medium	Bishop, Bakers
NIGGER	Semi-double	Eyeless	Mid	Medium	Blackmore & Langdon
SHEBA	Semi-double	White	Mid	Medium	Blackmore & Langdon
STARTLING	Semi-double	White	Mid	Medium	Blackmore & Langdon

VI. Well-spaced florets

CHAPTER VII

BELLADONNAS

*

IN the Belladonnas we have a breed of delphiniums quite distinct from the Elatums in form and habit, and noteworthy for the purity of their lovely blue flowers. For many years the progenitor of the race, *D. belladonna*, about whose origin very little is known, has been a popular garden plant. It was thought to be quite sterile, until early in this century Mr. Gibson, of Leeming Bar, succeeded in harvesting three pods of seed from which he raised five plants. Eventually two of these were put into commerce under the names of Grandiflora and Mrs. G. Gibson, and from these most of our present-day belladonnas have descended.

As might be expected from such a sterile parent, few of its descendants are fertile (Cliveden Beauty and Grandiflora are exceptions), and for this reason, up to the present time, less than 3 doz. varieties have been introduced. However, on rare occasions some Belladonnas do set a few seeds. I have harvested a number of seeds on Orion this year (1948), a variety that with me has never before been fertile. Breeders' attempts to cross them with the species or the Elatums have not, as far as I am aware, met with any success, the reason being that *D. belladonna* has forty-eight chromosomes, the species sixteen or thirty-two and the Elatums thirty-two.

These fairy delphiniums, or " Cinderellas of the Delphinium World " as they have so aptly been called, are widely grown in borders for their simple grace and charm. They do not dominate the garden with majestic spikes in the manner of their Elatum cousins, but their clouds of pure blue butterfly flowers, borne on slender branching stems, are incomparable for their elegance and beauty.

With a few taller exceptions, they range between 2 and 4 ft. in height, which makes them ideal for middle positions and towards the front of the border. As single plants they are not very effective, but are better planted 12 to 15 inches apart in groups of three or more, according to the size of the border and the effects desired. As a general rule I prefer using them in smallish groups as a foil to other flowers rather than massing them as prominent features. Careful planning is needed in arranging the groups to obtain artistic colour effects, and, since their colour range extends from pale Cambridge to deep purple blue, there is plenty of scope for the expression of individual taste in the grouping. The beauty of most border flowers is enhanced by being closely associated with these dainty delphiniums, and little imagination is needed to visualise many delightful arrangements. Pale blue and pink is a favourite combination, so Blue Bees, *Musis Sacrum* or *Semiplena* grouped with soft pink Phlox, Poppies, Clarkias, and many other flowers, cannot fail to give pleasure. For those who favour strong contrasts, a striking effect could be obtained by interplanting scarlet *Lychnis chalcedonica* and orange yellow *Heliopsis patula*, with the rich violet blue *D. Isis*. Many such combinations are possible, but these colour groupings are best left to each individual to arrange according to his or her own personal taste.

Belladonnas are simple plants to cultivate, and any garden soil where ordinary border plants thrive will meet their requirements. In preparing the soil only a moderate amount of farmyard manure or garden compost should be incorporated, since lavish feeding encourages a gross type of growth which is alien to their nature.

In their general cultivation the aim should be to develop the light graceful habit wherein lies their great charm, and, since they are naturally a bushy type of plant, no thinning is required as is customary with the Elatum varieties, but every shoot should be allowed to grow.

Staking is necessary for their support, but unless an unobtrusive method is employed their elfin beauty will be spoilt. Tying the individual stems to stakes can be very unsightly and the common method of encircling the group with canes, with string tied at intervals up the canes, is little better. The most satisfactory supports for such plants are short hazel branches (as used for green peas) thrust firmly into the ground and arranged lightly among the plants before they run up to bloom. The stems grow through the twigs and make tying unnecessary, so that nothing offends the eye since the branches are hidden by the foliage.

Whereas the Elatum varieties are mostly propagated by cuttings, division is the better method for Belladonnas. When additional stock is required, old plants, as soon as they break into growth in early Spring, should be lifted and divided into pieces with a few shoots in each and replanted at once into the border.

As cut flowers the Belladonnas are superb ; their light graceful racemes are ideal for table decorations and when artistically arranged in vases and bowls, either by themselves or in association with other flowers, they are delightful.

Although *D. Ruysii* Pink Sensation is not a true Belladonna variety it is grouped with them because of its similarity in habit. When first introduced in 1937 it met with a very mixed reception. But the public now realizes that this lovely salmon rose-pink delphinium is a fine garden plant and a charming cut flower, and the demand for it at the present time exceeds the supply. The new *D. Ruysii* variety Rose Beauty is likely to rival Pink Sensation in popularity. The colour is the same salmon rose-pink, but a shade deeper, and richer in tone, and although similar in habit its growth is more vigorous than Pink Sensation.

During the war nurserymen were obliged to reduce their stocks of plants to a minimum and in most private gardens flowers were sacrificed to make room for vegetables. Consequently, at the present time many Belladonna varieties are scarce, and some have disappeared from cultivation altogether. I have selected the following varieties as being the best of those now in commerce :

Arnold Böcklin. Deep lobelia blue, eye pale blue, height 4 feet. An attractive colour, the habit is good but in rich soil is inclined to grow rather tall.

Blue Bees. Pale forget-me-not blue, small bluish eye, 3 ft. high. Possibly the most popular of all the Belladonnas. In great demand as a cut flower.

Blue Dragonfly. French blue, eye pale mauve, height 4 ft., early flowering. A new variety raised by Mr. E. W. Mooring from a seedling × Blue Butterfly.

Blue Grotto. Deep Indigo blue, eye light, height 3 ft. A rich coloured, early flowering variety.

Capri. Brilliant sky-blue, light eye, height 4 to 5 ft. The origin of Capri and Moerheimi is interesting. A seedling from a blue parent had five flowering spikes, three with white flowers and two with blue. When propagated both came true to colour and were named Moerheimi and Capri respectively.

Cliveden Beauty. Cambridge blue, light eye, height 3 ft., considered to be an improved *D. Belladonna*, but the spike is rather thin. One of the few fertile varieties.

Dante. Deep violet blue, 3 ft. high. One of the newer varieties. In the same colour class as Isis and reputed to be an improvement on that variety.

Horatius. Cobalt blue with a slight pink flush, eye light, height 4 ft. Shares with Semiplena the distinction of being the only semi-double varieties.

Isis. Rich violet blue, eye light, height 3½ ft. One of the finest dark Belladonnas. A grand plant in the border.

Lamartine. Deep purple blue, eye light, height 4 ft. Another good dark variety. Fine branching habit.

Moerheimi. White. Height 5 ft. The only white variety, but it has a bluish tinge which gives it the effect of being somewhat dirty.

Mrs. J. S. Brunton. Brilliant sky-blue, eye light, height 4 ft. An attractive variety with a good branching habit.

Mrs. Thompson. Bright mid-blue, dark eye, height 4 ft. Very free flowering. One of the most popular varieties.

Musis Sacrum. Pale Cambridge blue, eye light, height 3 ft. A charming light-blue variety for decorative purposes.

Naples. Bright gentian blue, eye light, height 4 ft. A first-class border plant. Free flowering and a good branching habit.

Orion. Cobalt blue, light eye, height 4 ft. Vigorous habit and one of the best for cutting because of its long lasting quality.

Semiplena. Azure blue with a pink flush, eye light, height 2½ ft. Semi-double. No garden should be without this Belladonna, it is one of the loveliest front row border plants.

Theodora. Bright mid-blue slightly flushed rose, eye sepia, height 4 ft. Most attractive as a cut flower and a fine garden plant.

Wendy. Bright gentian blue tipped purple, height 4 ft. Very vigorous and an excellent branching habit. One of the most popular varieties.

D. Ruysii Pink Sensation. Salmon rose-pink, eye rose, height 3 to 4 ft. Mildew resistant. Charming as a border plant and indispensable as a cut flower.

D. Ruysii Rose Beauty. Deep salmon rose-pink, eye rose, height 4 ft. Mildew resistant. A more vigorous and deeper coloured variety than Pink Sensation.

CHAPTER VIII

SPECIES

*

AMONG the numerous delphinium species there are many charming plants worthy of greater attention than has been given them by the gardening public. Even among the members of the British Delphinium Society there are very few who cultivate to any extent these lovely wildings. Occasionally a few of the better-known species are to be seen at the Royal Horticultural Society meetings, and at similar exhibitions, but apart from these popular species the great majority of the wild delphiniums are practically unknown to ordinary gardeners. Admittedly there is much that remains to be done by the botanist to separate out the lesser known species, but there are many that deserve a place in our garden and on the Show table.

Probably one of the reasons for the lack of knowledge concerning these species is the difficulty of obtaining plants or seed in this country. The native homes of these delightful wild flowers are situated in every corner of the globe, although, strangely enough, none is a native to this country —nor can Australia give us any. Generally speaking, seed is only obtainable from collectors or from naturalists living in the district where the species is a native. The acquisition and cultivation of these dainty delphiniums is a fascinating hobby which is followed by a few enthusiasts. They spare no trouble in obtaining seed from every available source, and we owe much to them for the work they have carried out, since without their activities our knowledge of the rarer kinds would be very meagre indeed.

To be successful with growing species some attempt

should be made to provide the plants with conditions approximating to those prevailing in their native habitat. Although some adapt themselves readily to our climate, such as *D. tatsienense*, others, especially those from California, do not and must receive special treatment. Speaking generally, Europeans and Asiatic species can be dealt with as hardy alpines, some perhaps in scree˙; whereas those that hail from dry Levant or Syria, e.g. *D. Zalil*, need more care and attention. The Californian and more delicate Asiatics are best treated as half-hardy, the dormant roots being potted up and stored in a cool greenhouse or frame, and planted out at the end of May or early June.

Unfortunately many people are apt to compare the species with the modern monarchs of the border, clearly to the former's disadvantage, for, by comparison, some of the species may appear poor and dowdy, if one's taste has been vitiated by " overfeeding." But among these wild delphiniums may be found plants that, from the point of view of daintiness and beauty, would hold their own in any company, provided (and alas ! it is a big proviso) true seed can be obtained. And moreover it is to the species we must turn for our scarlet and yellow colourings in this genus.

My personal experience, apart from growing a few of the more popular species, is not wide enough to enable me to write authoritatively on the subject. I have, therefore, been obliged to glean much of my information from other sources. In the various records that have been consulted there is a lack of agreement regarding the details of some. For instance—*D. vestitum* is described by Farrar as having a white eye, but Clay says it has a dark eye. Also, *D. laxiflorum* is stated by Phillips to be 9 to 18 ins. high, whereas Nicholson gives it as 4 to 6 ft. These are only two of the many discrepancies that occur.

In the list that follows will be found most of the best-known species and a number of the rarer ones, but no attempt has been made to include them all. A complete list would run into possibly four or five hundred species.

It is improbable that seed can be obtained at the moment of many of the species mentioned, but it is hoped that collectors will be able to bring some into this country in the near future.

AFRICAN SPECIES

D. macrocentron. A tender hairy species from East Africa. Its drooping flowers are blue and green, sometimes yellow and green.

D. Welbyi hails from Abyssinia and is fairly hardy in Britain. Possesses clear soft pale blue flowers in its native haunts, which (alas!) are not always produced in captivity.

There is a pure white, but less hardy, variety known as *D. Leroyi.*

AMERICAN SPECIES

D. alpestre hails from the rocky places in Colorado. Stiff stalks about 6 ins. tall carry in July a few medium blue flowers with yellow eyes. The leaves are hairy.

D. Andersonii. A 3 ft. American and an improvement on many of the Menziesii clan, e.g. *D. columbianum.* Flowers bluish-purple.

D. azureum is a native of the North American Rockies and grows to a height of 3 ft. The plant has a branching habit, and in late May or early June it produces large sky-blue flowers.

D. Burkii. From California—height about 2 ft. Frequents riversides, and has indigo florets. Has a smaller cousin in *D. diversicolor.* The plant Farrar describes as *D. scopulorum* is probably *D. Burkii.*

D. cardinale is a Californian and needs a light soil in a hot corner of a well-drained garden. When given this it is

VII. Delphinium Ivy Ridgwell

a fairly robust creature, whose flowering stem, rising from rather succulent foliage, reaches over 3 ft. In August this stem is crowned with bright scarlet flowers which open out widely, unlike those of the frailer and poorer *D. nudicaule.* The roots are tuberous.

D. carolinianum is a beautiful species from North Carolina. Its flowers are of medium blue borne on 2 ft. stems. It has a white counterpart known as *D. Penhardii.*

D. carporum. This flower from the Rockies is a lovely creature. From a downy bunch of hairy leaves rises a foot-high velvety stem carrying a slender spike of white and pink flowers, each with a very pronounced " spur."

D. Cockerellii grows to a height of 4 ft. or more ; is a fine handsome species from South Colorado and makes a big bush from which rise the flowering stems. The blooms, though scanty, are large and of a bright purple. The foliage is gummy.

D. decorum. A deep blue or violet species with a yellow eye from California. Its 18 in. stems are graceful, and its florets are large.

D. distichum. From the damp and boggy meadows of the Rockies. Rather tall and erect with pale blue flowers.

D. Emiliae. A non-tuberous species from the Redwood region of West America. Deep blue flowers. Similar in habit to *D. grandiflorum.*

D. exaltatum. A synonym for *D. elatum.* A 3 to 6 ft. variety from North America. Blue flowers.

D. geraniifolium is yet another from the Rockies. It is a late flowerer with dark blue flowers on foot stems.

D. Geyeri. A poisonous variety from the Central Rockies and Colorado. From woolly tufts there arise stems some 18 ins. high, carrying azure blue flowers with a yellow eye. It is free-flowering and is particularly poisonous to cattle.

D. Hanseni. California gives us this free-flowering plant. The flowers are of a pinkish-mauve colour tipped with blue, but are not over attractive. Very similar to *D. hesperium*.

D. hesperium is very similar to *D. Hanseni*. It comes from Southern California and is said to be very tender. The flowers are a true blue, borne on stout $2\frac{1}{2}$ ft. stems. A white variety is fairly common ; also a pinkish variety, called *D. recurvatum*, is known.

D. leptophyllum. From the Mexican highlands. A good variety having deep blue blooms.

D. luteum has pale yellow flowers and is really *D. nudicaule var. luteum*.

D. Menziesii. A fleshy rooted American from California and the West Coast. Large mid-blue flowers are borne in July on slender 1 ft. stems. Patience is required to grow these from seed since the seeds usually take a year or so before germinating. It is closely allied to *D. decorum*.

D. Nelsoni is a Nebraskan variety. It is of the *Menziesii* group and very typical in every way. Stems about 6 ins. and flowers a downy blue.

D. nudicaule is a dwarf and weaker version of *D. cardinale*. In fact, it is one of Farrar's " miffs." The half-closed florets are scarlet in colour with yellow eyes. It is best grown in the moraine. Its native habitat is California. Some varieties of this are known, e.g. *D.n.var.* Chamois with apricot flowers, and *D.n.* Lemon Queen with pale lemon flowers. Height 1 ft.

D. Parishii. A brilliant blue member of the family from California. From scanty and almost hairless foliage spring stems of 18 in. or more, terminating in narrow spires of bright sky-blue.

D. Parryi. Yet another Californian whose flowers are larger than the preceding one, and for the most part of a deeper blue, though purple and white varieties are known. It grows some 2 ft. in height and flowers April to June.

D. scaposum comes to us from the dry places in the Southern Rockies and so it needs first-class drainage and heat. The leafless stem of some 2 ft. carries a dark blue raceme of flower.

Very near to this are *DD. amabile, confertiflorum, xylorrhizum.*

D. scopulorum is to be found by the sides of mountain streams in California. It is closely allied to *D. elatum* and grows some 4 ft. in height. Its flowers are of an indigo blue and its finely divided foliage is rather glaucous, but probably the correct name of this plant is *D. Burkii.*

D. simplex. More tuberous rooted than *D. scaposum*, but otherwise very similar except that it grows some 3 ft. The florets are blue with a white eye. It comes from the mountains of Idaho and Oregon. It has remarkable browny-black seeds and white wings.

D. tricorne is found on the Atlantic coast of North America. It is the eastern counterpart of the western tuberous rooted *Menziesii* class. After blooming in the spring the tubers ripen off in the summer as though they were dead. The florets are larger and of a rich blue with a white eye. It is about 9 ins. in height and has a docile temperament.

D. trolliifolium, as the name implies, has foliage that resembles the *Trollius*. It comes from moist places in the Columbia River valley and is of easy culture. Growing about 1 ft. in height, in April it bears half-closed white-eyed florets of dark blue.

D. vimineum. This plant from Texas is probably a variety of *D. carolinianum.* It grows 3 ft. in height and has brilliant azure florets on branching stems from July to September.

ASIATIC SPECIES

D. altissimum grows in the highest places. A Himalayan hairy plant of graceful branching habit some 3 ft. tall. Flowers blue and purple.

D. biternatum. Larger but not so good as *D. Zalil*—flowers a paler yellow.

D. brunonianum is a 9 in. rather squat plant from the high alps of Tibet. The queer dusky purple flowers are large and well formed and hooded rather like a monk's cowl. In its native habitat it has a strong musk scent, but when grown in the British Isles the scent is not so noticeable. Its beauty is only revealed by lifting the bell-shaped cup, the inside of which has a lovely hairy centre, curiously marked with a bluish shade.

D. cashmirianum. A most desirable dwarf from Kashmir and suitable for the rock-garden, growing as it does about 10 ins. high. The flowers are normally light purple but white varieties and lighter blue ones are known. There is also a much dwarfer variety of this, known as *D.c. var. Walkeri* which has light-blue flowers with yellowish central petals.

D. cheilanthum. A 3 ft. variety from Siberia having dark-blue florets with pale yellow eyes borne on erect branching stems.

D. coelestinum comes from eastern Szechuan and is one of the glories of the race. It is a 4 ft. variety, its leaves are very finely divided and its branching spikes are of brilliant azure blue, the individual flowers being loosely arranged.

D. coeruleum. A species from Sikkim and Tibet. Barely 1 ft. high it has light branching spikes of Cambridge blue flowers. An excellent plant.

D. dasyanthum. From the screes of Alatan. Large flowers of brilliant blue, short downy spur. 1½ ft.

D. Davidii. One of the tall ranunculus-leaved varieties from Eastern Tibet. 3 ft. spikes of real blue.

D. Delavayi. A 10 in. dwarf from Yunnan. The stems are hairy and the florets bright blue. A particularly good plant for the rock garden.

D. Fargesii. From Szechuan. This plant makes 1 ft. tall

pyramids of brilliant dark blue flowers. The spurs are hairy.

D. formosum. This is a doubtful species and may be only a variety of *elatum*. It has handsome foliage from which rise some 2 to 3 ft. spikes of violet-blue blossom. Altogether a graceful plant.

D. Forrestii is a curious member of the family and practically the same as *DD. densiflorum* and *pellucidum*. The flowers are pale and water blue—slightly veined purple.

D. glaciale. From the heights of Sikkim where each plant produces a few large hairy blossoms on a 9 in. stem. Mid-blue in colour, smelling of musk.

D. hybridum. Flowers blue with two lower petals bearded white. Racemes covered with florets with straight spurs longer than the flowers. Flowering June to August. A native of Tauria. Growing 3 to 4 ft. high.

D. laxiflorum usually grows about 12 ins. and comes from the Altai Mountains. Somewhat like the European *D. dicty-scarpum* but with larger flowers of pale blue. The leaves are leathery.

D. likiangense. To be found in the limestone screes and pastures of Yunnan. The flowers are large and borne several together in short racemes. In cultivation these flowers are soft blue pale, but in their natural state Forrest describes them as " brilliant clear rich blue with the same sweetness as Roman Hyacinth." Height 1 ft.
Very near to it are *DD. Beesianum, calicola, candelabrum* and *labrangense*.

D. nanum has long-spurred blue flowers and is probably an annual.

D. orthocentron. A very near relative to *D. tatsienense*. Pale blue long-spurred flowers on branching 1½ ft. stems. A native of Sutchuen.

D. Przewaldskyi. A pale yellow variety, sometimes tipped blue, from Mongolia. Height 1 to 2 ft.

D. Pylzowii. This species is found in the Kansu province

of China. Its branching racemes are crowned with bluish-white flowers. Height 1 ft.

Very near *D. likiangense*.

D. Soulei. A pygmy from the dry places of Szechuan. A hairy downy spike of 6 ins. stands above a bunch of smooth green leaves and bears a crowd of blossoms whose upper petals are pale blue and the lower ones dark.

D. suave. A beautiful species from Kurrum Valley in Afghanistan. The 10 in. stems carry a number of large pale blue flowers with the two lower petals creamy white.

D. sulphureum. Another annual masquerader under the name of *Zalil*. A pale yellow in colour and not so good a plant as *Zalil* it comes from Syria. Of branching habit and height 4 ft., it flowers late in the summer.

D. tanguticum. Another pygmy, only 4 ins. in height, that comes from Szechuan. The flowers are somewhat like *D. caucasicum*, but larger, more free-flowering and a richer violet in colour.

D. tatsienense (often incorrectly called *tatsiense*). Probably the most popular of all the species and yet another of those that comes from Szechuan. An elegant branching plant 12 to 18 ins. in height producing in summer long spurred pure cornflower blue flowers, but, alas! it is not too hardy and, as Farrar says, " has a way of sometimes vanishing like the Snark softly and silently away."

D. tibeticum has deep blue flowers on a slender stem about 2 ft. in height.

D. triste. A 2-ft. variety from Siberia. The spurs are violet but the flowers are dark brown suffused with red at the edges of the sepals.

D. tsarongense. Somewhat like *D. likiangense*, but produces much larger flowers—in fact the largest flowers of all. They are a watery blue or green in colour and are veined, fragrant and hairy. It is hard to distinguish from many others, e.g. *DD. glaciale* and *chrysotrichum*, though *glaciale* as a rule has smaller flowers and in *chrysotrichum* the hairs are more golden and outstanding. It is found across the East from Armenia to the Chinese alps.

D. vestitum. From the high Himalayas is a superb creature. It is quite easy and flowers in August or early September when most delphiniums are over. The spikes are some 4 ft. in height and covered with deep violet flowers with a dark eye.

D. yunnanense. A bright blue variety with a brown eye, long slender spurs and straggling habit. From China and Tibet. 2 to 3 ft.

D. Zalil. The true species is a gem from Afghanistan and of different class from *DD. sulphureum* and *ochroleucrum*. It is a true perennial of robust constitution and its flowers are a brilliant yellow with orange markings. It is tuberous rooted and grows to a height of 3 ft., flowering in late summer. Let me quote Farrar on it, for he says, " The flowers are a brilliant yellow, so brilliant indeed that all the rolling meadows and downs about Gilran are an undulating sea of gold when it is in bloom." Other writers say that Farrar's imagination ran away with him, and that the real colour of *D. Zalil* is " pure sulphur yellow with orange markings." The flowers are used in Persia for dyeing silk.

EUROPEAN SPECIES

D. ajacis. This is the common larkspur and is to be found in English cornfields, especially round Cambridgeshire. It is not a native of this country but probably came from Europe, where it is common. It is a 3 ft. annual with blue and other coloured flowers. The name is derived from the supposition that the letters AJA can be seen in the lines of the petals of the flowers.

D. cardiopetalum. A Mediterranean annual which grows about 1 ft. high. The racemes are covered with blue to purple florets.

D. caucasicum. A little gem from the Caucasus, as the name implies. It is barely 4 ins. high with leathery hairy leaves. The flowers are borne on single stems and are a lovely clear blue with purple outside and white eyes.

D. consolida. An annual from Northern Europe. The racemes are few flowered and are loosely built, varying from purple to white in the original type, but many rich colours are now obtainable.

It is sometimes confused with *D. ajacis.*

D. dasycarpum. A soft blue variety from the Caucasus, with dark brown petals. Very close to *D. elatum.* It grows 4 to 6 ft.

D. devaricatum. A popular blue annual from the Caspian and Caucasus. It has small flowers on slender stems.

D. dictyocarpum comes from the Caucasus. The flowers are borne on leafy stems, have a straight spur and are pale blue in colour. Height 2 ft.

D. Duhmbergii. A 6 ft. fellow from Russia with blue and white flowers. Flowering June to August.

D. elatum is the common delphinium of the Alps. It is to be found universally on the stony slopes, and is the forefather of our lovely border varieties. Its natural colour is corn-flower blue, and it can be grown anything up to 6 ft. in height.

D. fissum. A blue slender-spiked variety from Transylvania growing to a height of 3 ft. and flowering from June to September.

D. Freynii is a dwarf variety from the Caucasus. Less than 1 ft. in height with a thick 3 ins. spike of intense blue.

D. grandiflorum. A grand species from Russia, Siberia and China. Often called the " Siberian Larkspur." Some 2 ft. in height and of a dark blue colour, it is a worthy plant and is adaptable to English gardens. *D. sinense* (often called, erroneously, *chinense*) is but a synonym for this plant, though perhaps it is found more proliferous than *grandiflorum* itself.

VIII. Modern blue seedlings

Several varieties are known, e.g. Blue Butterfly and Blue
Gem. Yet another variety is that known as *D. cineraria
coeruleum*. Set in a light sandy soil rich in humus, it makes
a gem for the front of the border, with its upturned
spurless chalices of pure Cambridge blue. 8 ins. high.

D. ochroleucum is often sent out by tradesmen, erroneously,
as *D. Zalil*. This variety which comes from the Caucasus
and Levant, is probably only an annual and is a poor
thing compared with the true *Zalil*. Its elongated racemes,
crowned with lemon yellow florets, reach some 2 ft. in
height.

D. oxypetalum. A pale blue dwarf species from Central
Europe some 9 ins. in height.

D. Requienii. A biennial from south-west Europe, and,
synonymous with *D. pictum*, it grows 2 ft. high, has
branching stems and its florets are bluish-white with pink
and green markings.

D. staphisagria. A poisonous biennial from Southern Europe
whose florets are a reddish-purple. 2 to 3 ft.

D. tenuissimum. A Grecian variety with loosely built panicles
of violet-blue. 1 ft.

CHAPTER IX

BREEDING

*

BREEDING new varieties of flowers is one of the most fascinating branches of horticulture. There is an absorbing interest in cross-fertilizing one variety with another, and then growing the resulting seedlings and watching them day by day as they come into bloom. If a variety of outstanding merit appears among the seedlings, the thrill is unequalled by any other gardening experience.

It is beyond question that the results achieved by cross-fertilization are far greater than can possibly be obtained by haphazard saving of seeds. When seed is gathered from named varieties there is every probability that many other people are saving seed of the same varieties, consequently there is little chance of turning up anything really distinctive. But by cross-fertilizing one variety with another, if it is carried out intelligently, success sooner or later is fairly certain. It is, however, essential for the breeder to have a definite idea of what he wishes to accomplish, and not to cross varieties in a haphazard fashion, which usually leads nowhere. When selecting varieties for parents he should always keep in mind the characters he wishes to develop in his seedlings and see that these characters are very strongly marked in at least one of the parents. The seedlings resulting from the cross—known as the first filial generation, or F_1 for short—after the obviously bad ones have been eliminated should be self-fertilized. The F_2 generation should then be grown, and the same procedure followed the next year and the F_3 generation grown. It is also a good plan to " back-cross " some of the most promising seedlings, that is, cross-fertilize them with the original parents. The result of this systematic breeding will be that the desired types will gradually emerge.

There is a wide field open to any one with sufficient enthusiasm wishing to take up breeding delphiniums, but instead of endeavouring to improve existing Elatum varieties, let him make a new start with the species. There are plenty to choose from, and without a doubt new forms could be evolved. It would be a long quest, with many disappointments, but nevertheless, a worthwhile undertaking, and one crowded with interest. Some of the lines awaiting the hybridist are the development of yellows from *D. sulphureum* and *D. Zalil*, of reds from *D. nudicaule* and *D. cardinale*, and new blues from the numerous blue species. There is also unlimited scope for breeding among the Belladonnas, of which there are few varieties. Pure blue varieties of the " *semi-plena* " type would be eagerly welcomed, as would a wider range of colours in this section.

Any one with the necessary enthusiasm and time to take up this great work of hybridizing would of necessity have to become thoroughly acquainted with the science of breeding, known as Mendelism. But to those who have no intention of practising breeding beyond raising a few seedlings by cross-fertilization, a serious study of Mendelism is not imperative ; all that it is necessary for them to know is how to carry out the operation of cross-fertilizing. All the same a knowledge of the general principles of Mendelism is an undoubted advantage.

Those who are not familiar with the process of fertilizing delphiniums should take a floret and pull it into pieces and so become acquainted with its formation. First take out the centre petals that form the eye (Fig. 4). Grouped in the centre of the floret, behind the eye, are the sex organs, known as " pistils " and " stamens." The pistil is the female organ, consisting of the ovary, or seed pod, which contains the ovules, or embryo seeds. At the apex of the ovary is a

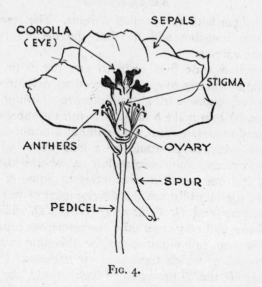

FIG. 4.

hollow stem called the "style," at the tip of which is the "stigma." This is the receptive organ for the male pollen grains. Delphiniums usually have three pistils, but occasionally there are more. Surrounding the pistils are the male organs, known as "stamens," consisting of "anthers," which have the appearance of a dozen to twenty tiny black knobs borne on slender stems. These contain the "pollen" grains, which are the male germ cells. Individually the pollen grains are far too small to be seen by the naked eye, many thousands being carried by each anther which, when it bursts, has the appearance of being coated with exceedingly fine white powder.

The time for fertilizing a delphinium floret is when it is about to open. At this time the stigmas become receptive and the pollen grains are ripe for reproduction. The anthers burst, and shed their pollen grains on the stigmas. At this receptive period the stigmas become slightly sticky so that the pollen grains adhere to the tips, where they, in a manner of speaking, take root and send out tubes, which grow down the styles to the ovaries and fertilize the ovules.

When a flower is fertilized by its own pollen it is said to be self-fertilized, but when pollen from a different variety is used it is cross-fertilized. It has been suggested to me, quite seriously, on more than one occasion, that I might raise yellow delphiniums by crossing them with buttercups or some other yellow flower. This, of course, is quite impossible. A flower can only be fertilized by another flower belonging to the same family. Flowers from different families cannot be mated together any more than can dogs and cats, or horses and elephants.

It will be obvious that to carry out the act of cross-fertilizing the flower that is to be the seed parent must be emasculated, that is, the anthers must be removed to prevent the stigma being self-fertilized. This is a delicate operation which must be carried out with the greatest care, for any damage to the pistils would render them incapable of being fertilized. In the first place the floret must be examined to see that none of the anthers has burst. If there is the slightest sign of white pollen on any of the anthers the floret must be rejected and another selected not so far advanced. In removing the anthers a pair of forceps, or finely pointed scissors, are useful. I frequently use a small pocket-knife for the purpose, but would advise the use of scissors or forceps for a beginner, because with these they would be less likely to injure the pistils. Having emasculated the floret the next step is to pollinate it with pollen from another variety. This is done by picking a fully expanded floret with ripe pollen from the variety selected as the male parent, and carefully removing the petals that form the eye. Then with the lightest possible touch convey the pollen grains to the stigma by contact. This is much better than using a camel hair brush. Pollination should be carried out immediately the florets have been emasculated. If the florets are in a receptive condition some of the pollen will adhere, but should it fail to adhere, pollination should be repeated the following day. The middle of the day is the best time for pollinating. A magnifying glass is useful for examining the stigmas to see if the pollen has taken, as it is not always possible to see it with the naked eye.

Labels with details of the parentage should be tied on the pedicels of the pollinated florets, putting the seed parent above and the pollen parent below, thus :

LADY ELEANOR
X
BLUE BEAUTY
28-6-47

The date of the cross should be included. Full details should then be entered into a notebook. By such means the pedigree of the varieties raised can be traced.

It is generally recommended that flowers that have been cross-fertilized should be enclosed in muslin cages to prevent interference by bees and various insects. It is a safe policy, although I have never found it necessary with delphiniums. I have, however, been obliged to tie the seed pods in bags to protect them from tits and wrens who will rip open seed pods by hundreds.

When the seed pods turn brown and before they begin to burst they should be gathered, placed in paper bags and hung in a sunny window where they will ripen in a few days. If the crosses are made in June, the seed will be ready for sowing by the end of July. It is better to sow the seed as soon as it is ripe rather than keep it until the following Spring. Thus a better germination will take place.

Although cross-fertilizing flowers needs patience and a considerable amount of care, most keen gardeners can carry it out successfully if they master the fairly simple technique. But they must not lose sight of the fact that being able to cross-fertilize flowers is only the first step in the art of breeding, and little real progress can be made without some knowledge of the laws of inheritance. It is not possible in the space available to give more than a very brief outline of the way in which characters are inherited, but I will endeavour to explain in simple language the principal points of Mendelism, although some technical terms must unavoidably be used.

Gregor Mendel was born in 1822 of Austro-Silesian parents. At twenty-one he became a monk, and later was made Abbot of Brünn. He was interested in various branches of science, particularly in the problems of breeding. By a series of experiments he discovered the laws of heredity, but it was not until the beginning of this century that the great value of his discovery was appreciated.

Mendel carried out a number of experiments with garden peas, choosing pairs of varieties that bred true for certain characters, such as smooth and wrinkled seed, green and yellow seed, tall and dwarf habit, etc. and, selecting a number of these differentiating characters, investigated their heredity separately for each character. In one series of experiments crosses were made between tall and dwarf peas, varieties being used that bred true for these characters. The plants resulting from the cross, known as the F1 generation, were all tall. Because only the tall character appeared in the F1 generation, Mendel called it the " dominant " character and applied the term " recessive " to the dwarf character. The flowers of the F1 plants were then self-fertilized and the resulting plants grown the following year. In this F2 generation both tall and dwarf plants appeared, but no intermediates ; there were, however, three times as many talls as there were dwarfs. That is—the characters that appeared in the F2 generation were 3 dominants to 1 recessive. Self-fertilized seed was then saved from each individual tall and dwarf plant of the F2 generation and grown the following year, this was the F3 generation. From seed saved on the dwarf plants, only dwarfs were produced, which shows that the recessive character breeds true. Seed saved on the tall plants gave a different result ; only a proportion bred true to the tall character, the others producing both talls and dwarfs in the proportion of 3 talls to 1 dwarf, showing that the tall plants of the F2 generation were of two kinds—those that carried the tall character only, and those that carried both the tall and dwarf characters. The former were called pure dominants and the latter impure dominants. By breeding further generations Mendel proved that the pure dominants and recessives always breed true, but the impure dominants produce as offspring pure dominants, impure dominants and recessives in the constant proportions of 1—2—1.

Mendel's Law as applied to Tall and Dwarf Peas

T   Tall (breeds nothing but Tall)
T_1 Tall (breeds Tall and Dwarf)
D   Dwarf (breeds nothing but Dwarf)

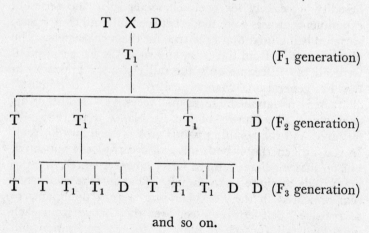

and so on.

IX. Delphiniums as a cut flower

So far only one pair of characters—tall and dwarf—has been considered, but each pair of the many thousands of characters concerned with the building up of a complete plant, or animal, is controlled by the same laws of inheritance. Each pair of characters, however, acts independently of the other pairs. For instance, if a tall variety with wrinkled seed were crossed with a dwarf variety with round seed, both of which bred true for these characters, the seedlings resulting from the cross would be tall peas with round seeds, because tall is dominant over dwarf, and round is dominant over wrinkled seed. The recessive characters would appear in the F2 generation in the proportions before mentioned. It is, however, a much more complicated matter when dealing with hybrid flowers that do not breed true to any character. In this category are Delphiniums, Lupins, Phlox, Chrysanthemums, and many other plants. Breeders of these flowers make it their business to observe the dominant and recessive characters of the flowers they are raising, and the measure of their success depends largely upon applying this knowledge to the best advantage.

All these plant characters are conveyed from one generation to another in the germ cells by what may be called atoms of heredity, known as " Genes." Genes are exceedingly small, in fact too small to be seen, even by the aid of the most powerful microscope ; but even so, much is known about them and the way they function. Each individual one of the thousands of characters concerned in the identity of a plant, such as height, scent, resistance to disease, size of flower, leaf shape, season of flowering, to name only a few, is controlled by a gene. It is obvious therefore that every germ cell must carry many thousands of genes by means of which all the characters of a plant are passed from one generation to another in the process of fertilization. Although a gene, as a rule, is mainly concerned with a particular character, it is quite usual for it to have an effect on several other characters ; also for a particular character to be affected by several genes.

The reason the progeny of hybrid plants, such as delphiniums, vary in colour, size, shape and in many other ways both when self-fertilized and when cross-fertilized, is because the male and female germ cells carry differentiating characters. For example, one may carry the gene for large and the other for small flowers. But when the two germ cells carry identical characters then there is no variation in the progeny, as in wild flowers and other plants that breed true when self-fertilized.

As a result of the fusion of the two germ cells in the act of fertilization a new body cell is formed containing a pair of each of the numerous genes which control the characters of the two parents. The new body cell, by a process of division, develops into a seed which grows into a plant containing in every body cell the two sets of genes complete.

By the aid of a very powerful microscope a cell can be seen to consist of an outer wall, lined with a thick film of a transparent semi-fluid substance, known as " cytoplasm," contained in which is a denser globular body. This is the " nucleus," which may be regarded as the brain of the cell. The remainder of the cell is filled with cell sap. Careful observation reveals that the nucleus consists of a number of threads that resemble strings of beads. These are the " chromosomes " which actually are chains of genes. Although the genes themselves are too small to be seen, the containers in which they live, known as " chromomeres," are visible, joined up like beads on a necklace. The genes always occupy the same positions, and are arranged in the same sequence in the chromosomes. In every body cell of hybrid elatum delphiniums are sixteen pairs of chromosomes of varying shapes and sizes in haphazard arrangement, one of each pair having been supplied by the female parent and the other by the male.

When the new cell, that has been created by fertilization,

begins to grow, a change takes place in the nucleus. The chromosomes, which at first had the appearance of strings of beads, now contract, growing shorter and thicker until they look like short rod-like bodies. Then they move to positions across the middle of the cell and each chromosome splits lengthways into halves, making two sets of thirty-two chromosomes. After the division has taken place the two sets separate and move to opposite ends of the cell, a membrane grows around them and a wall grows across the centre of the cell making two cells where previously there was only one, with a complete set of identical chromosomes in each. These cells develop to their full size and the whole process of cell division is repeated. In this way a plant grows by the division of its cells, each body cell containing a complete set of genes inherited from its two parents.

When germ cells are being formed there is a difference in the manner of cell division, resulting in germ cells having only sixteen chromosomes instead of thirty-two like the body cells. This is brought about in the following manner. The chromosomes, one from each parent, are paired up, lying closely side by side, with the related genes directly opposite each other, instead of being grouped in a haphazard manner as in body cells. (Related genes are those that control the same characters.) The chromosomes then contract, move to the centre of the cell and separate, as they do in body cell formation. But, and this is the important point, they do not split into halves—with the result that the complete chromosomes go to the opposite ends of the cell, sixteen to either end. For this reason it is called reduction division. Thus it will be seen that the chromosomes from the male parent and those from the female parent are always distributed to different germ cells, and consequently two related genes are never passed to the same cell. When the pairs of chromosomes are lying close side by side an important movement of the genes takes place which has an effect on variation in the progeny. The movement is known as

" linkage "—or crossing over. The pairs of chromosomes break into pieces and an interchange of corresponding portions takes place. This results in a mixture of the genes from the two parents being passed on to the new germ cells.

Although only the fringe of the subject has been touched, sufficient has been said to give would-be breeders a little idea of the ordered way in which characters are transmitted from one generation to another. But for those who wish to make real progress in plant breeding a serious study of the subject is necessary, and the following books are recommended :

PRACTICAL PLANT BREEDING, by W. J. C. Lawrence.

MENDELISM, by R. C. Punnett.

THE CHROMOSOMES, by M. J. D. White.

THE GENETICS OF GARDEN PLANTS, by M. B. Crane and W. J. C. Lawrence.

I would recommend beginners to read them in the order given, for the first of these is less technical and more easily understood than the last two.

11. D. Audrey Mott, a fine modern variety

VIRUS DISEASE CUCUMIS I

12. Showing two spikes of same variety—one infected, the other healthy

13. Leaves from above plants. In infected leaf note narrow and long pointed segments compared with healthy leaf

CHAPTER X

DELPHINIUMS IN THE BORDER

★

THE Delphinium is undoubtedly the aristocrat of border plants, and highly though it is esteemed as an exhibition flower because of its wonderful form and colouring, it is as a garden plant that it reigns supreme, and adds such beauty to our herbaceous borders. What more beautiful sight is there than a well-planned border with its riot of colour and succession of flowers? But where would that border be without the shades of blue and mauve that the delphinium supplies? Blue is the favourite colour of so many people, but it is also the rarest in our border plants. The Delphinium, therefore, comes into its own and is practically without a rival in this range of colours. This fact, combined with its towering spikes and the beauty of its florets places it in the very forefront of hardy plants.

In the border it can be used with great effect by careful grouping with other flowers, and although, sometimes, a haphazard planting may prove very effective, it is far better to plan carefully the arrangement, taking full account of colour, height and flowering period, whether early, mid-season or late. Since delphiniums range in height from $3\frac{1}{2}$ to 8 or 9 ft. they are most useful in breaking up any suspicion of "flatness," which would ruin the artistic effect of any border. But a word of warning might not be out of place here. When selecting delphiniums for the garden do not allow yourself to be influenced by the spikes you may have seen on the show table. Many a variety that is ideal for exhibition purposes is not necessarily good in the garden. Whereas exhibitors are mainly concerned with plants that will produce large and perfectly built spikes, the gardener, when planning his border, should select the more robust and free flowering types. Since "garden" growers of delphiniums far outnumber those who grow them for exhibition purposes, it is a matter of much importance as to which are the more suitable varieties for the purpose. Many a gardener has condemned the whole race because he has failed to produce the blooms he expected, but how many times has it been his own fault in selecting varieties which are only suitable for the show table?

From what has been said it must not be assumed that all exhibition varieties are necessarily bad border plants. On the contrary, many are well suited for that purpose, but some definitely lack the stamina and hardy habit needed to make them ideal garden plants. Let us examine, therefore, some of the qualities that are essential in a really good " border " delphinium. First of all, it must be robust— a variety that has proved its robustness over a number of years. Then there is the form and spacing of the florets. To bring out the full charm and grace of the spike, these florets must be so spaced on the stalk that the individual beauty of each is revealed. On the ideal spike the florets should be slightly separated from each other. They should not be packed so closely together that their petals overlap to any extent, for if the overlap is at all excessive the beauty of the flower is spoilt in that it becomes a mere mass of colour.

Height is another feature that must be considered, and considered carefully. Very tall varieties are undesirable, except to be used occasionally in back positions. The taller the variety the harder it is to support the blooms; and even with the most skilful staking they are ever liable to be damaged by strong winds. The dwarf varieties are excellent for forward positions, but few are available at the present time. There are, however, some pure blue "dwarfs" coming on to the market in the very near future.

In planning a border many facts arise to which careful

consideration must be given. There is, firstly, its position. The selected site should get plenty of sunshine and an abundance of air. It should be well away from tree roots, which would rob the plants of moisture and nutriment, and should be quite clear of overhanging branches, which would tend to draw the plants up unduly. The protection of a hedge on the windward side (but not too close) is a decided advantage, especially if the border is at all in an exposed position.

In gardens where space is plentiful the herbaceous border, being usually only one of many features, should be planned as an integral part of the whole lay-out ; but where space is limited, and this applies to the majority of gardens, the most satisfying results can be obtained by making the border the principal feature.

As to the design, this depends largely upon the size and shape of the space available, but speaking generally a bold and curving outline is the most effective. Such a design gives varying depths to the border and makes it possible to utilize the widest spaces for planting imposing groups. Moreover, it adds greatly to the setting if the border can be bounded by a well-kept lawn. Due thought must be given to the effective grouping of the plants and their con-trasting colours. Many a border has been spoilt because the gardener has not given thought to his colour scheme or time of flowering, for continuity of bloom is of the utmost importance. Plants must be so placed that large flowerless spaces are avoided, and as one group fades another must be at hand to take its place.

As the border under consideration is particularly for delphinium lovers, and those who wish to make this flower the dominating feature, the grouping of these plants must be the first consideration. It is unnecessary, however, for me to recommend particular varieties, for all the information that can be desired will be found in the Delphinium Society's Register. Here will be seen details as to height, colour and time of flowering. Also those varieties which have gained awards at the Wisley Trials. With the Register before him no gardener need fear to make his own selection.

Let us assume, then, that a scale plan of the border has been made and that the desired space has been allocated to the delphiniums, both tall and short, early flowering and late, not forgetting the Belladonnas. How else is the border to be filled ? Once again individual tastes must play their part, but the early spring display must come principally from bulbs, though I know many people prefer not to have bulbs in a hardy plant border. Without them, however, it would indeed be bare in the early part of the year. So let us have some Daffodils, Tulips, St. Brigid Anemones, Polyanthus and Primroses to cheer us up after the drab winter months.

There are some hardy plants of outstanding merit which, when in flower, dominate the border. Such are the varieties of Iris Germanica, and Lupins in early June, Delphiniums in June and early July, Phlox in July and August, Gladioli in August and September, early Chrysanthemums and Michaelmas Daisies in late summer and autumn. Their numerous varieties cover a wide range of colours, and they should be liberally distributed throughout the border to ensure continuity of bloom. For instance, if Michaelmas Daisies have been planted among or around the Delphinium groups, when the latter are over and cut down the former will be coming into flower, and so a large bare patch will be avoided. Or again, " Madonna " Lilies or Lilium Regale, liberally planted, are splendid companions to Delphiniums. Many other plants readily suggest themselves as " fillers in " to our border—for back positions Anchusas, the taller Heleniums, Heliopsis, Verbascums and so on ; for mid-positions the selection is too numerous to mention, and for the front of the border, if one wishes a change from such things as Anthemis, Nepeta, Iceland Poppies, and Pyrethrums, why not try groups of annuals ? Or let me strongly urge the inclusion of some of the dainty dwarf delphinium species particularly *D. tatsienense* and *D. grandiflorum*, Blue Butterfly. These could not fail to please even those gardeners whose tastes are most fastidious.

CHAPTER XI

DELPHINIUMS UNDER GLASS

*

AMONG the outstanding features at the R.H.S. Chelsea Shows are the superb groups of greenhouse grown delphiniums exhibited by Commercial Specialists. It is often a matter of wonder how these can be had in bloom a month before their normal time. The cultivation of delphiniums under glass presents no great difficulty provided the best method is followed and suitable plants are selected.

The first essential is a well-ventilated greenhouse, or conservatory, fully exposed to the sun. High temperatures are not required, since anything in the nature of forcing would be disastrous ; but sufficient heat must be provided to keep the night temperature above 40° F. In the early months of the year heat will be necessary to keep the day temperature in the neighbourhood of 60° F. Good ventilation is of vital importance. In the daytime, except in extremely cold and bad weather, full air should be given, but the ventilators should be closed for the night before the sun leaves the house.

Success with delphiniums in pots depends largely upon having very vigorous plants with plump basal eyes. The earliest struck cuttings usually make the best plants for the purpose. As soon as the cuttings are well rooted they should be potted into 3 in. pots and, before they are pot-bound, potted on into 4½ in. pots, and then into 8 in. pots, in which they will remain until the end of the year.

A compost that will give first-class results is known as the " John Innes " potting compost. It consists of :

7 parts good fibrous loam
3   „   granulated peat
2   „   coarse sand

all of which should be measured by bulk.

Add to this $\frac{3}{4}$ oz. ground limestone, chalk, or hydrated lime per bushel of compost, and $\frac{1}{4}$ lb. "John Innes base" per bushel of compost. This latter consists of :

2 parts Hoof and Horn ($\frac{1}{8}$ in. grist)
2   „   Superphosphate of lime
1   „   Sulphate of Potash

all parts being measured by weight.

A good crock drainage is essential in the large pots, and the soil should be firmly rammed round the edges of the pots. After potting, they should be plunged to the rims in ashes in an open position in the garden where they will remain until the end of the year ready to be brought into the heated greenhouse in January.

To encourage the growth of basal shoots the small bloom that develops on the young cutting should be removed, and when the new shoots are growing strongly all but one should be cut off at the base. This shoot should be allowed to bloom, and since any further flowering would be detrimental to the quality of next season's flowers, a few pods of seed should be allowed to ripen on the spike as a restraining influence on the dormant eyes at the base of the plant.

When the 8 in. pots are full of roots, daily watering will be necessary, and an application of weak liquid manure every seven days will supply the nutriment required to build up vigorous plants. For feeding pot plants a special manure has been compounded for use in conjunction with the John Innes potting compost. This "J.I. Feed" is sold in two forms, "L" for liquid and "D" for dry feeding. After the plants have flowered the feeding should be discontinued. Little attention other than watering is needed at this season since they will be dying down for a period of rest. As the plants become dormant watering should be eased off, but they should not be allowed to become quite dry.

At the beginning of January the plants should be brought into the heated greenhouse. Although they will produce reasonably good flowers if they are grown on in the 8 in. pots, better results will be obtained if at this time they are potted on into 10 in. pots, using the same compost as before, but with the addition of ½ lb. of the John Innes base manure per bushel of compost instead of a ¼ lb., as used in the previous potting. At first great care must be taken not to over-water them. It is only when the pots are full of roots and the plants are growing vigorously that they may be watered more freely and feeding with liquid manure can begin. The amount of nutriment contained in an 8 or 10 in. pot is quite inadequate for supporting a delphinium, and unless the plants are fed regularly the results will be disappointing. In my opinion frequent applications of weak liquid manure give better results than strong doses at long intervals. So I advocate a feed of quite weak liquid manure once every seven days, and this will be sufficient until the bloom spikes become visible. Then, as the spikes begin to develop, instead of increasing the strength of the manure, apply it at the same strength every four days until the blooms show colour, when it can be discontinued.

The number of stems that should be grown on the plants is a matter of personal preference. When specimen blooms are desired the plants should be thinned to one spike per plant, but for decorative purposes three moderate-sized spikes may be preferred. The thinning should take place when the plants are 6 to 9 ins. high.

As soon as the bloom spikes begin to lengthen staking will be necessary, and since neatness is particularly desirable in pot culture, 4 ft. green bamboos should be used for the purpose, and green twist for tying. To keep the plants healthy full ventilation must be given in the daytime whenever the weather is favourable, especially during sunny periods when the temperature of the house rises rapidly. At such times it is very beneficial to create a damp atmosphere by watering the floor around the plants. Most varieties respond well to greenhouse treatment, although some colours become more delicate in tone. This is particularly so with the pure blue varieties.

The Belladonnas, including Pink Sensation, are also suitable for pot culture, but in their case the preliminary potting is unnecessary. They should be lifted from the open ground at the beginning of January, potted into 7 in. pots and taken straightway into the heated greenhouse. The same treatment should be given to them as to the other varieties. Growing delphiniums under glass is beyond the reach of most ordinary gardeners, but those having the facilities would be well repaid for their trouble by the joy of having delphiniums to decorate their house during May, when flowers usually are so scarce.

CHAPTER XII

DELPHINIUMS FOR DECORATION

*

THE Delphinium is not one of the best of flowers to use for decoration indoors, but it does not deserve the wholesale condemnation that is so often given to it. Admittedly it does not last long in water and the petals soon drop and litter the floor or carpet, but if selected varieties are used it will be found to be not too unsatisfactory.

Little use can be made for decorative purposes of those giants often seen on the show table, or of the towering spikes of the border, but even these have their uses in such places as concert halls, or churches which have to be decorated at wedding times. Provided the space is large enough and of goodly proportions the largest delphinium spikes can be used with great and pleasing effect. Even in the home, the hall and lounge can be made gay with a bowl of large spikes standing in a corner.

To produce the thin-stemmed elegant type of spike, which is most suitable for decorative purposes, it is best to grow the plants in a plot of the garden by themselves, and instead of restricting them to four or five stems a dozen can be grown on each plant, and the feeding for border plants advised in a former chapter is unnecessary.

When choosing delphiniums for decorative purposes, only those with long-lasting qualities are worth considering. Many varieties when in bloom begin to drop their lower petals long before the top of the spike is in flower. Such varieties, no matter how lovely they may be, are of little value for decorating. Some, however, last in water much longer than others. William Richards for example—a dainty sky-blue variety, with quite small flowers and slight, elegant spikes—probably keeps better than any other variety. Audrey Mott is another ; even on the largest exhibition spikes, the lower florets of this variety are retained until the topmost flowers are in bloom.

Lateral spikes are useful for decorative purposes, and if full advantage is to be taken of these, a plant or two should be " sacrificed " by cutting out the main spike when it is a few inches long. By so doing the strength of the plant is thrown into the laterals, making them much finer than they would have been had the main spike been allowed to fully develop.

It seems to be a common belief that the life of cut flowers can be prolonged by adding such things as aspirin or other chemicals to the water, but so far as I can say from personal experience, nothing of this nature has any effect. Some types of bloom fade quickly if their stems are not treated in some way so as to allow the water to flow freely up their stalks. Of such are those with " woody " stems like the Michaelmas Daisy, or the Chrysanthemum. These should have the end of their stalks crushed with a hammer or split with a knife. The same trouble occurs with hollow stemmed flowers such as Delphiniums, especially if they are cut in the heat of the day. But this disadvantage can be overcome with a little care, as the following personal incident will illustrate. I was staging an exhibit on the eve of a show of the British Delphinium Society and not far away was a lady arranging a vase of Belladonnas. They were perfectly fresh and she soon had them arranged ready to be judged next day. When she arrived the next morning, however, her flowers were in a state of complete collapse and were hanging over as if they had been out of water for days. She asked me to come and look at them. When I suggested that cutting the stems under water would revive them she said, " What's the use of that ? " and in disgust she took them out of the vase and threw them under the staging. I asked if I might experiment with one, and putting a spray in a pail of water, I cut off some 2 ins. under the water, leaving the stem in the water without exposing it to the air. We stood talking for some minutes when she turned and caught sight of her flower. She stared at it in amazement for it had revived, and then exclaimed, " It's a miracle." She hurriedly treated the other discarded blooms in the same way and once again set up her exhibit. Later I observed she had been awarded second prize.

It is advisable, therefore, to treat all decorative Delphinium spikes in this way and so avoid that air lock which often forms in hollow stemmed flowers if exposed to the air. This airlock prevents the water from flowing up the stem, and as soon as the water which is in the stem has been used up the flower collapses. By cutting the stem under water the airlock is removed and the water syphons up in a normal manner.

Care should always be taken in the selection of the vase that is to be used for decoration. It is essential that one of tall and ample proportions should be used, and an artistic effect is obtained when the spikes are so arranged that they carry on, as it were, the outline of the vase. The vase itself should be inconspicuous, neutral in colour and quite plain. Glass vases are not desirable since they show the stems. When decorating for the house usually only one aspect of the vase is meant to be seen, so ideas can be concentrated on that aspect ; but it must be remembered that, when exhibiting, the judges are very liable to examine the exhibit from every angle and allowance must be made for this in the arrangement.

If a " mixed " vase is under consideration, care must be taken to select flowers that blend well with Delphiniums. Generally speaking, flowers of a similar build, that is to say, " spiky flowers," will go better with them than those of a different type, such as roses for example. For foliage use should be made of the gracefully curving side spikes of delphiniums before they come into flower.

One of the chief problems in the arrangement of delphiniums is to know how to keep the thick stems in position. When using a vase I have found a very efficient method is to fit a large-mesh grid over the top of the vase and to place a crumpled ball of large-mesh wire in the bottom. By this means the stem can be held in two places. For basket decoration bowls or jars should be fitted into the baskets with crumpled large-mesh wire fixed firmly in them so that it cannot move. This method is preferable to that of using glass " arrangers " which only hold the flowers in one position.

For table decoration there are few flowers so charming as the Belladonnas. Their light, graceful sprays are admirably suited to this purpose, and although most people prefer a decoration of one colour very pleasing effects can be obtained by combining, say, *Pink Sensation* with the pale blue *Musis Sacrum* or *Semi-plena*. The small side-shoots of the elatum varieties can also be used for this purpose. But why not depart from the beaten track and use some of the dwarf species ? Why not get some seeds, say of *D. tatsienense* and grow them—and they grow so easily—for this purpose. I can assure you a daintier flower for table decoration cannot be found. There are several others which would equally well fill the bill ; *D. grandiflora* for instance, or any of its varieties. Another method of table decoration —and one which, as far as I know, has not been greatly explored—is to use individual florets stripped from their spikes. For this method it is best to use florets with exceptionally long pedicels. The cornflower blue Agnes Brooks is an ideal one, and a table decorated thus will never fail to please.

Let me end with a word of warning. A common fault in flower decoration is overcrowding, particularly in vases and baskets. The aim of every decorator should be to produce a light and graceful arrangement.

CHAPTER XIII

EXHIBITING

*

A LITTLE over a century ago Napoleon regarded us as a nation of shopkeepers. To-day it would be truer to call us a nation of gardeners, since there are comparatively few people in Britain who do not practise gardening in some shape or form. It is a hobby that is pursued by young and old, rich and poor, with great enthusiasm, particularly by those who concentrate on growing flowers of the highest quality for exhibition at Horticultural Shows. Exhibitors are small in numbers compared with those who grow flowers for garden adornment only. Nevertheless horticulture owes a great deal to Exhibitors and the Specialist Societies they have created, since much of the progress that has been accomplished in breeding new varieties, and in improved methods of cultivation, is due to the encouragement given by these Societies and to the zeal of their exhibiting members. The Delphinium is a grand flower for exhibition, since no flower responds more readily to good treatment. Moreover it is well within the ability of most people to grow blooms of the size and quality required for successful showing, provided they are prepared to give their plants a little more than ordinary care and attention.

Having made the decision to cultivate delphiniums, the intending exhibitor would be well advised not to rush in too soon to show his flowers. It is far better to wait a season and to visit the British Delphinium Society's show in order to become acquainted with the points that make an exhibition spike. He should study the first prize exhibits comparing them with the unsuccessful ones, and endeavour to judge for himself in what way one has succeeded whilst the other has failed. All the useful data that can be gathered should be entered into a notebook for future reference. This should include details of varieties, especially novelties, noting their outstanding qualities and defects. By keeping such records and making a critical study of varieties, a store of knowledge of great value to an exhibitor is built up.

To grow delphiniums of the quality required for exhibition more specialized cultivation is needed than has been recommended for garden delphiniums. Provided they are healthy and vigorous garden delphiniums may be left undisturbed in the border for several years ; but for exhibition purposes finer blooms are produced on plants grown for one year only. These are grown from cuttings struck early in the year, and, after they have produced their show blooms the following year, are destroyed and replaced by new plants. Too much stress cannot be laid on the importance of commencing with vigorous cuttings, because it is essential to build up very strong plants with healthy roots and plump eyes before Winter sets in. These vigorous yearlings, with judicious feeding, will produce spikes of a size and quality that will hold their own in the keenest competition. The cuttings should be struck as early as possible. Those struck in heat in January are best, since they have an advantage over later cuttings of the few weeks extra growth. When they are rooted there are two different methods of dealing with them. The first is for large gardens where two plots can be devoted to exhibition delphiniums, one plot for the current year's show blooms, and the other for planting with rooted cuttings in May for the following year's flowers. In the autumn the plants that flowered in June are destroyed and the ground prepared for re-planting with cuttings the following May.

In small gardens, however, where exhibition delphiniums have to be grown in the same positions year after year, a different plan should be followed. Early in July, as soon as the show blooms have been cut, the plants should be dug up and destroyed and the ground deeply dug and manured immediately, so that a new batch of plants can be planted at the earliest possible moment.   It is of the utmost importance to have the planting completed before the end of July, for unless the plants gain a firm hold of the soil and make very good growth before they die down for the winter, there is little hope of them growing into the fine vigorous plants so essential for the production of first-class show spikes. Only the strongest plants should be used for July planting, and every effort must be made to grow them from the beginning without a check. As soon as the cuttings are rooted and hardened off, they should be transplanted 9 ins. apart into a temporary bed where they will remain until their permanent places are ready in July. They should then be lifted with a large ball of soil so that there is a minimum of root disturbance, and set with their crowns about 1 in. below the surface of the soil, which should be well firmed with the feet all around the plants, followed by a thorough watering.

An alternative to transplanting the cuttings into a temporary bed is to grow them on in pots. It is a satisfactory method that can be adopted by those who have no available space in the garden for transplanting. The cuttings when rooted are potted into 3 in. pots, moved into $4\frac{1}{2}$ in. pots, and finally into 7 or 8 in. pots, which are stood on ashes in an open place fully exposed to sunshine. More attention must be given to plants in pots than to those in the ground since they need watering every day during hot weather. Therefore any one not prepared to give them constant attention should not attempt the pot method. By July the large pots will be full of roots and the planting out should not be delayed beyond the end of the month, otherwise their roots will become pot-bound and the development of the plants seriously affected.

In preparing the ground deep cultivation is essential, but

14. Cross-fertilising by hand, showing emasculated florets in centre of spike being pollinated

15. Packing spikes for exhibition

it is not necessary to dig more than a depth of 2 ft. Nothing different from the details given in the chapter on " Ground preparation " is needed, except that a more liberal quantity of farmyard manure should be incorporated. Also where there is the slightest suspicion regarding the acidity of the soil a test should be made. If found to be acid the correct amount of lime to raise the pH to 6·5 should be applied.

Drastic thinning is necessary for the production of show blooms. On old plants two or three spikes can be grown, according to the vigour of the plants, but on yearlings, as a general rule, only one spike should be allowed. If the plant is very vigorous then two may be permitted, particularly on those that are inclined to grow coarse or fasciated stems. After they have been thinned a mulch of half-rotted farmyard manure spread for 2 ft. around the plants will not only nourish them but will keep the ground cool in hot weather and help to prevent the evaporation of moisture.

No matter how well the soil has been prepared, no matter how much manure has been incorporated, nor how fine are the plants, first-class show blooms will not result unless the plants are fed. A weekly application of a balanced fertilizer will add very considerably to the length and breadth of the spike and to the size of the florets. Feeding should commence about the end of April, or early in May, when the plants are 18 to 24 ins. high. At this time the stems are swelling, and, although not visible, the blooms are developing in the heart of the shoots. Everything possible must now be done to stimulate the plants into vigorous growth. Stimulants are best supplied in copious draughts of liquid fertilizer, weak at first but gradually increasing in strength as the plants gain in stature. Give them sufficient to penetrate to the full extent of their root run, applying it not close against the stems, but for fully 2 ft. around the plants. There are several prepared complete manures on the market suitable for this purpose, " National Growmore " for example. For

T.D.   I those who prefer to mix their own fertilizer the following mixture is recommended. Superphosphate of lime 2 parts, Sulphate of potash 1 part, Nitro Chalk, or Sulphate of Ammonia 1 part. This should be applied at the rate of ½ oz. per gallon of water for the first two feeds and increased to ¾ oz. per gallon as the plants grow stronger. Each plant should receive two gallons of the mixture every ten days until the bottom florets show colour, when feeding should be discontinued. Fertilizers should not be applied if the soil is dry. When such is the case the plants should be watered with plain water the previous evening. It is an advantage to change the feeding occasionally, and an organic manure such as " Peruvian Guano " may be used, if it can be obtained. Some growers find feeding with liquid manure too strenuous, and prefer to apply the fertilizer in dry form. This is quite efficient provided it is well washed in with a hose pipe, or is applied during rainy weather. But whichever method is followed the feeding must be regular, otherwise the results will fall short of the highest standard.

Of the various ways that show spikes can be staked I prefer using 5 ft. bamboo canes ⅝ in. thick with carnation tips inserted in the tops as described in an earlier chapter, each spike being supported by a separate stake. Care must be taken to see that the spikes are tied clear of the stakes so that no damage can occur to the florets by strong winds blowing them against the canes. Occasionally it will be found necessary to adjust the canes as the blooms develop, and sometimes as the show time approaches additional canes will be needed to safeguard the blooms during squally weather. Usually there are far too many lateral blooms on the spikes, so some of them must be disbudded. This should be done as soon as they are large enough to break off with the thumb and forefinger. The topmost laterals are the ones to remove, leaving about four of the bottom ones. On no account should all the laterals be disbudded. The British Delphinium Society is very particular on this point and has drawn up the following recommendation as a guide for exhibitors. " The Committee recommend that delphiniums should be staged with three or more laterals attached. Therefore, all other points being equal, spikes exhibited with laterals will take precedence over those without any."

Having grown the flowers, even if they are of front-rank quality, the battle is not yet won. There is much to be done needing care and skill in gathering, transporting and staging them before the grower can have the satisfaction of seeing his exhibit decorated with the coveted 1st Prize card. Of the many operations connected with exhibiting flowers staging is one of the most important, since much depends upon placing them before the judges, artistically arranged and in faultless condition. It is by no means uncommon for an exhibitor who has grown flowers of the highest quality to be beaten at the show because of his lack of skill in staging his exhibit.

Entries usually have to be sent in several days before a show, and beginners may experience difficulty in deciding how many and which spikes will be available. It will be found that most varieties are ready for exhibiting about seven days after the first floret comes into bloom. The time varies a day more or less according to the weather. A considerable amount of valuable time can be saved on the show morning if the spikes for each class entered are selected before they are cut. The name of the variety and the number of the class in which it is being exhibited should be written on a tally and attached to each spike. This selection is only provisional, because at the show there is little doubt that some re-arrangement will be necessary, but a preliminary selection will save confusion when the flowers are being staged.

If the weather is dry a good watering given to the plants a day or two before the spikes are cut will improve the flowers and help to keep them fresh while travelling. They should be cut either late in the evening or early in the morning, allowing sufficient time for the dew on the flowers to dry before they are packed. The spikes selected should not be fully out ; those that are in bloom right up to the top of the spike are liable to drop their lower florets before they are staged. Judges will not penalise spikes with 6 ins, or even more, of unopened buds at the top, but they will not consider those that are shedding their bottom petals. Strip off all the foliage except the top half a dozen leaves and cut the spikes about 6 ins. from the ground. They should then be loosely arranged in deep vases of water and stood in an airy room or shed with the windows open. Before putting the spikes in the vases the stems should be filled with water. To do this invert each spike and fill the stem with water from a jug, place a fingertip over the end of the stem to prevent the water escaping, and then gently turn the spike the right way up and place it in the vase. Great care is needed when turning the spike upright as owing to the weight of water in the stem it is liable to break unless supported by the hand in the middle of the spike. The result of filling the stems is that they remain full of water while they are in the vase and the flowers do not wilt while they are in transit to the show. The water must be allowed to drain out of the stems before they are packed.

When the spikes are being cut, it must not be overlooked that some of them may begin to drop their florets before they can be staged, so a number of spares must be taken. These should be fresh young flowers, especially young if the weather is very hot. In hot dry weather flowers that are in the pink of condition overnight may shed their petals next morning before judging time.

A number of clean fresh delphinium leaves should be gathered for finishing off the tops of the vases after the spikes are staged. Nothing makes an exhibit look more untidy than to see wads of paper and pieces of stem, that have been used for fixing the spikes into position, projecting from the tops of the vases. Four or five leaves will hide this necessary packing and help the decorative effect of the exhibit. A supply of pieces of delphinium stem should also be taken for fixing the spikes in the vases. The stumps left when the spikes are cut are just right for the purpose, being much better than the wads of paper used by many exhibitors.

Transporting spikes to the show is one of the delphinium exhibitors biggest headaches. I well remember the anguish I experienced when conveying some spikes to one of my earliest shows. I firmly fixed deep vases in boxes and stood the flowers upright in water in a motor van. The spikes were tied to canes and were securely wedged in the vases, but the canes did not reach quite to the top of the spikes. This was my undoing. For as soon as the van got to an uneven part of the road the tips of the spikes began to whip backwards and forwards and first one and then another tip broke, so that scarcely a spike remained with a sound top by the time we reached London. The most distressing part of the affair was that I was sitting in the van with the flowers and had to watch the tops break, being quite unable to do anything to prevent the damage. On arrival at the show I neatly repaired them with stub wires, hoping they would escape the judge's eye. I learned from this experience that spikes travelling upright must have their tips supported, either by being tied to canes, or by the spikes being wrapped in tissue paper. The usual method of transport is to pack the flowers in shallow wooden cases. The spikes, each wrapped in tissue paper, are packed close together so that there can be no movement ; the stems at the bottom being steadied by stiff rolls of newspaper laid across them. Although the flowers become somewhat crushed, they soon recover when placed in water.

For short journeys instead of packing them in boxes they can be laid two deep on the floor of a motor van, the floor being covered with soft paper and the spikes packed side by side close enough to prevent them moving. On arrival at the show they should be placed in water immediately so as to revive them. The ordinary green pottery exhibition vases are not suitable for this purpose since they are easily over-balanced, so exhibitors should take suitable receptacles with them. At the British Delphinium Society's exhibitions the R.H.S. provide vases for staging the spikes. For single spikes the smallest vases are best, but when two or three have to be shown in one vase the largest size should be used. Exhibitors who grow large spikes with very thick stems may have difficulty in persuading three to go even into the largest size provided so they would be well advised to take their own vases for the " three in a vase " classes.

It is important when staging either two or three spikes in a vase to arrange them so that they can be seen to the greatest advantage. Keep in mind the fact that it is the defects rather than the good points for which the judges will be searching. It behoves the exhibitor therefore to display the best flowers in prominent positions where they will catch the judge's eye, and keep poor ones in the background. When one spike is being shown nothing can be concealed. Of course the best side must be shown to the front, but it is fairly certain to be turned round by the judges and any defects it has will be seen, so flowers, as nearly perfect as possible, should be selected for single spike classes. But with three spikes in a vase, especially in nine or twelve spike classes, by carefully arranging the flowers some defects can be hidden. For instance, where one of the three spikes has seed pods forming or a gap low down in the spike, it can be placed in the centre at the back of the vase and the other two arranged in front with their laterals screening the defective flower.

In six and twelve spike classes with " two in a vase " the pair for each vase needs careful selection. They should be similar in type and approximately the same height. A broad pyramidal spike shown in the same vase with a long cylindrical one, no matter how good they are individually, would spoil the artistic arrangement of the whole group. Also with " two in a vase " it is better not to mix dark and light varieties in the same vase. In classes where there are " three in a vase " a different arrangement can be made. A tall spike can be placed in the centre with shorter ones on either side ; also, regarding colour arrangements, a dark spike between two light ones or vice versa looks very well. Whether the centre spike is placed in front or behind the two side ones depends upon the quality of the flowers. If it is a very fine flower place it in front where all its good qualities can be seen, but if it is a little the worse for wear place it behind.

When the best spikes have been staged it is sometimes difficult to select the best of those that remain. Never forget that freshness is of outstanding importance, and that size, by itself alone, is no recommendation. A big one must be a *good* big one. A smaller spike of good quality should always be chosen in preference to a larger one of indifferent quality. When staging by the side of a strong competitor put your best flowers next to your opponent's. Should you have a better spike than his of any particular variety place it as near to his as possible, so that the judges will be influenced in your favour by the comparison. Naturally it follows that if he has a spike of a variety definitely superior to yours keep yours as far away as possible, or better still substitute one of another variety.

And lastly, always make a point of arriving at the show with your flowers in good time, since a good exhibit cannot be staged in a hurry. Successful exhibiting depends so much upon careful staging, so it is folly for exhibitors, who have spent a whole year in growing good flowers, to throw away their chances of success by allowing insufficient time for a proper arrangement of their exhibits.

GLOSSARY

*

Anther	That portion of the male organ of a flower which contains the pollen and is situated at the top of the stamen.
Back-cross	Crossing a hybrid back to one of its parents.
Belladonnas	A race of delphiniums mostly derived from the hybrid variety D. Belladonna.
B.D.S.	British Delphinium Society.
Chromomeres	The houses in which the genes live.
Chromosomes	Rod-like bodies contained in the nucleus, carrying the genes in linear arrangement.
Cross fertiliza-tion	The act of putting the pollen of one flower on to the stigma of a flower of a different variety.
Cytoplasm	A thick film of semi-fluid substance which lines the outer walls of the cell.
Elatum	From Latin " elatus "—meaning tall. The name given to the race of garden hybrids derived from the Alpine species D. Elatum and many others.
Eye	The corolla. A cluster of petals in the centre of the floret.
Floret	An individual bloom.

Genes	Tiny specks of living matter that control the growth and development of plants and through which characters are transmitted from one generation to another. They are arranged linearly in the chromosomes.
Hybrid	A plant resulting from crossing two species.
Linkage	The movement which takes place and effects the offspring when pairs of chromosomes are lying side by side.
Mendelism	A theory of heredity demonstrated by Gregor Mendel, an Austrian monk.
Nucleus	The collection of chromosomes contained in each cell.
Ovary	That part of the flower which contains the immature seed.
Ovules	The immature seed.
Pedicel	The short " stalk " on a floret.
Petal	Small flower leaves forming the corolla or eye of the floret.
pH	A symbol denoting the acidity or alkalinity of the soil, thus pH1, pH2, etc.
Pistil	The female organ of the flower.
Pollen	The male fertilizing dust-like powder from the anthers.
R.H.S.	Royal Horticultural Society.
Self-fertilization	An act of putting the pollen from a flower on to the stigma of a flower of the same plant.

Sepals   The flower leaves forming the floret, commonly called petals.

Stigma   A female organ of the flower at the tip of the pistil which receives the pollen.

Stool   A plant from which cuttings and " splits " are taken.

Style   That part of the pistil between the stigma and the ovary.

INDEX

*